Middle East Realities

Understanding the Conflict

Oliver James

PublishAmerica
Baltimore

First printing

At the specific preference of the author, PublishAmerica allowed this work to remain exactly as the author intended, verbatim, without editorial input.

ISBN: 1-4241-3928-7
PUBLISHED BY PUBLISHAMERICA, LLLP
www.publishamerica.com
Baltimore

Printed in the United States of America

This book is dedicated to my young grandchildren,
Emmett James, Luke Timothy and Sofia Amber,
with the hope that they will grow up
in a world of peace, justice and harmony.

Table of Contents

List of Maps

Foreword

Before reading this book, I'd like to provide you with the credentials I have for writing it. I am not an academic or historian. Nor am I a politician or lobbyist. For over 55 years I have been an observer...but an up close observer. I was born in Kentucky of Lebanese immigrants. I went to high school at the American University of Beirut and was in Lebanon during the UN partition of Palestine in 1947 and the 1948 war that ensued. After university in the U.S. and a stint in the army, I returned to Lebanon for six years as an employee of Middle East Airlines, the local Lebanese air carrier. Later, working for an international petroleum company, I spent two tours in Saudi Arabia totaling eight years; the first during the Khomeini revolution next door in Iran in 1979 and the second during the first Gulf War in 1991. In between, I was in Brussels with responsibility for our company's business in the Middle East and Africa. During these periods of residence and tours of service, I had many occasions to meet and often befriend a broad spectrum of business people and government officials, from the highest to the lowest levels. My exposure has predominantly been from the Arab perspective. I want the reader to understand this. However, I believe my views are balanced and my objective is to provide historical context and fact and not so much personal opinion. Should personal opinions that I do harbor seep in I trust they will reflect my desire for a just and lasting resolution to a conflict that has raged much too long and impacted far too many people. If I succeed in this, I will be well pleased.

Oliver James

Prologue

Every being and every entity has a clear and defined reality. However, it is not this reality that shapes people's attitudes and drives their actions. Rather, it is the perception they have, which may or may not accurately reflect that reality. Over the course of time, the perceptions that peoples of the East and peoples of the West have acquired of each other have so developed based on the series of events observed and experiences encountered and by the fear or comfort, the distrust or delight that these engendered. Perceptions of another's culture, its political and economic systems, its religion and social order are all factors in the formulation of an attitude which may be favorable or unfavorable, enticing or repelling, friendly or unfriendly. And once formulated a perception seems increasingly difficult to alter. On the contrary, happenings seem to be interpreted in ways that reinforce a perception long held. Inconsistencies are deemed irrelevant and explained away and only those factors that support an earlier perception are accepted as validation. With centuries of conflict between civilizations the task of bringing people together in respect, acceptance and tolerance of one another becomes a rather enormous but extremely important undertaking. It must start with trying to understand. This book is dedicated to that essential objective.

Introduction

A noted historian once said that we study the day before yesterday in order that yesterday may not paralyze today and today may not paralyze tomorrow.

Yet history seems to teach us that we don't really learn much from history, or at least our actions seem to belie that adage. Maybe history simply foretells the consequences of actions we are bound to repeat today and regret tomorrow. We seem destined to duplicate the same mistakes over and over again, the price of which meanwhile escalates far beyond any measure of inflation.

We read much today about the looming clash between the civilizations that inhabit this planet. The severity of the conflict is yet to be determined but that a conflict exists there seems little doubt. But why? What has transpired in our histories that have so shaped our attitudes and perceptions that we today are poised on the threshold of yet another great, possibly violent, divergence? What are those events in our past that have so poisoned the present and now threaten our future? To name a single cause would be tidy but also rather naïve. There are probably a host of significant historical events which have disrupted peaceful coexistence between nations and civilizations, each such event reinforcing the other, magnifying and multiplying at each step the intensity of that hostility. Religious fervor, political rivalry, economic competition and cultural diversity have all been important components leading to envy, mistrust and a good deal of misunderstanding. It is good to remember that civilizations as such are not discreet political entities. They do not in themselves formulate foreign policy or wage wars. But the political entities that do are influenced and driven by the civilizations in which they thrive—or languish. So, while we may speak of a clash between the Islamic East and the Christian West we are really referring to the political regimes which best or more vocally represent them. As we proceed it is good to remember the words of Arnold Toynbee, the noted historian, who said civilizations tend to die of suicide, rarely by murder.

While by no means the only determinant, the perceptions we have today of one another are heavily influenced by a series of historical epochs, some of modest bearing and others more significant. I will deal only with those which were probably more influential and best remembered. The rise of the Islamic Empire in the seventh century is no doubt a good place to start, followed by the Christian Crusades of the thirteenth century, the Ottoman Empire in the fifteenth century, European colonialism after World War I and the rise of superpower imperialism. The object of this review is not to examine each in any great depth but rather to highlight them for the sake of understanding their role in the shaping of perceptions that exist even to this day.

One might easily argue that the alienation between Arab and Jew started with Isaac and Ishmael, half brothers and both sons of Abraham. Isaac, the father of the Jewish people, was the second son of Abraham, born of his aging wife, Sarah. Ishmael, who is considered the patriarch of the Arab peoples, was born of Hagar, Sarah's maidservant. Concerned that Ishmael might inherit from his father, Sarah prevailed on Abraham to banish both Ishmael and Hagar from their household. They wandered aimlessly through the wilderness of Beersheba and were close to death when the Lord appeared and provided them with water and the promise that Ishmael would also father a nation. (Genesis 21:18, 19) This Biblical context is one of many events that may have contributed, at least in some way, to today's bitterness. There are others.

The Islamic Empire

The Islamic Empire had humble beginnings. A young Arab of modest means, born in the city of Mecca in 570 AD, orphaned at a young age, began making regular trips to Jerusalem from Mecca with his guardian uncle as part of a caravan of merchants plying their trade between those two points and places in between. Mohammad was probably influenced by his exposure to and contact with both Jews and Christians and grew convinced of the existence of a single all-powerful, all-merciful God. It is said that through a vision he received from the angel Gabriel he was called to preach the message of one God to his countrymen who worshiped many gods or no gods, admonishing them to turn away from their lawless and wicked ways. He began by preaching his revelation in his hometown of Mecca, but when rejected and persecuted, he fled to Medina, a smaller city less than 200 miles to the north. This flight to Medina, in 622 AD, is significant as it marks the start of the Islamic lunar calendar. Parenthetically, many scholars do not believe that Mohammad actually started out to set up a new religion. His aim was simply to turn his people away from the worship of idols and to recognize the one and only one God.

In Medina, Mohammad attracted a dedicated following and found himself head not only of a budding new religion but also of a zealous community, legislating law and establishing order. From Medina Mohammad began his conquest of Arabia in the name of Islam. His followers were people who had found new light, a new beginning replacing tribal loyalties with the "Umma", a broader community of believers. They were on fire, full of zeal, completely confident and fearless in battle. The movement grew and became ever more powerful and more aggressive. Mohammad's successors, called Khalifas or Caliphs, were no less fervent and carried their message of one God far and wide and beyond the borders of Arabia. As they expanded they encountered two types of people. Pagans were given the choice of conversion to Islam or facing the sword. On the other hand, so-called "People of the Book", that is, people who already believed in one God, people who already had a 'revealed' religion—Christians, Jews and Zoroastrians—were given a different kind of choice. For the payment of a poll tax they could continue to freely practice their own religions and receive protection of the state. There seems to have been a degree of tolerance in those early times greater than exists in some Muslim countries even today. Bernard Lewis in his book *The Middle East* points out that the Syriac and Coptic Christians exchanged one dominating master for another and found Islam less demanding and more tolerant. Early Islamists believed that every Muslim, regardless of race, descent or social status, was equal in the eyes of Allah (God) and of fellow Muslims. However, such tolerance and equality was not extended to women, slaves and infidels, who did enjoy certain rights albeit of a much inferior nature. It should be noted that in this regard the Islamic religion was really no different than early Judaism and Christianity.

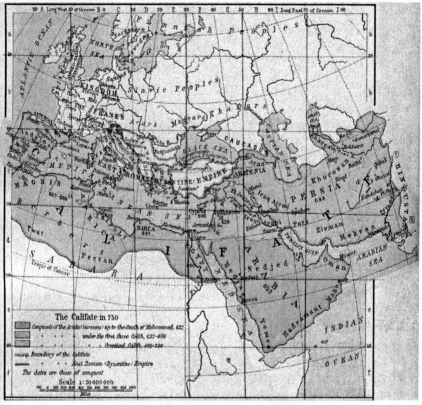

The Islamic Empire - 750AD
Courtesy of the University of Texas Libraries

As the Muslims expanded their Empire they were rather careful not to destroy or frustrate the institutions of learning and cultural promise they encountered. On the contrary they built upon what they found, encouraging the arts and sciences. Great advances were made in astronomy, mathematics, medicine, architecture and many other fields. They put to effective use numerals that had probably been invented in India, and the numbering symbols we use today are referred to as 'Arabic numerals'. Algebra and algorithm are Arabic words. Many stars have Arabic names thanks to the work of early Arab astronomers. They developed techniques for alloying metals and testing their purity and Al Hazen's published work on mirrors and lenses is still consulted.

In a relatively short time the Islamic Empire developed into an advanced civilization rivaling that of the Greeks and the Romans. The empire was expansive and diverse, stretching from northern India across North Africa and into Spain, threatening the heart of Europe. The empire spanned a period of 400-500 years from the seventh to the eleventh centuries. The eventual breakup of the empire was probably predictable and inevitable. Its strength eventually became its weakness. The empire was extremely diverse encompassing a wide mix of ethnic and cultural groups with parochial interest and differing aspirations. It was also split internally into two major divisions with the Shiites advocating the Khalifa, the secular and religious head, be selected based on the direct bloodline from the Prophet and the Sunnis advocating a selection process based on consensus. This division did not seem to inhibit early expansion and advancement, and is apparently more significant and divisive today than it was in those early times.

The Islamic Empire was so dispersed geographically that communication and transportation were understandably extremely slow and most cumbersome. In time, central control became virtually impossible, particularly with the rise of various regional military autocrats who created their own loyalties and set up their own autonomous quasi-states. There was also an economic dimension that contributed to the demise of the Islamic Empire. For a variety of reasons lucrative trade with China and countries on the northern borders withered away, negatively impacting the solvency of the Empire. International trade routes were diverted around the Middle East, with transoceanic vessels swinging around the Cape of Good Hope in southern Africa. The Islamic leaders were unable or unwilling to assimilate the rapidly evolving technological advances of Europe and were squandering an inordinate amount of their dwindling revenue on weaponry and military adventures.

It was during the eleventh century that influence from the capital in the East began to measurably weaken. Rival caliphates were set up and parts of the empire began to break away, eventually to be succeeded by another with greater zeal, more energy and unfettered by the bonds of complacency.

Inevitably, the very existence of the Islamic Empire over such a long period and the menacing nature the empire posed for Europe and other peoples on its fringes created centuries of fear and mistrust—that might diminish with time, but not be forgotten.

The Christian Crusades

Another significant event and contributor to the growing fear and mistrust between peoples of the Islamic world and those in the west were the crusades, which began at the end of the eleventh century. The publicized intent of the crusades was to free Jerusalem from Muslim rule. However, many believe that its genesis was as much political as it was religious. Alexius Comnenus, Emperor of the Byzantine Empire became fearful of the power and influence of the Muslim Caliph in Baghdad and, perhaps, his political designs on the Byzantine Empire. In order to deflect attention from and to frustrate any attacks on his own dominion, Emperor Alexius convinced Pope Urban II of the importance to Christians of recovering Jerusalem from Muslim rule. Interestingly, there seems to be no record of the Jews or Christians in Jerusalem experiencing persecution or being inhibited from worshiping freely until the Seljuk Turks occupied the Holy Land in 1000's and began impeding Christian pilgrims who wanted to visit the holy places. Nor is there record of a request for any such liberation. Nevertheless, this cause assumed broad appeal with Pope Urban II, perhaps holding promise of greater unity in the Christian church while enhancing the power and influence of the papacy. At the Council of Clermont in 1095 the Pope enlisted the support of churchmen and noblemen to 'free

Jerusalem' who then went out and spread their enthusiasm for a crusade throughout Europe. Some European states and principalities that were asked to participate no doubt saw it as a way to reduce domestic strife at home and, perhaps, to divert attention from their own failed policies. There were, for sure, large numbers of crusaders who were indeed zealous and saw themselves as defenders of the Christian faith. Others were adventurers and seekers of wealth with dreams of rich bounties or new markets.

There were a total of eight crusades spanning 174 years. The first crusade began in 1096 and Godfrey of Bouillon did indeed succeed in capturing Jerusalem in 1099, massacring Muslim and Jew alike. It was lost again in 1187 at the hand of the army of Salah-el-Din, never again to be regained by the Crusader armies that followed. The Holy Roman Emperor, Frederick II did succeed in negotiating another brief interlude of control over Jerusalem from the Sultan of Egypt. Until its brief loss in 1099, Jerusalem had been in Muslim control for over 400 years. It remained again under Muslim rule until 1922 when it became a mandate of the British Empire. By the 13th century the crusades had degenerated into intra-Christian feuding and even wars. The crusades never achieved the lasting goal of Christian rule over Jerusalem. Their success in Europe in converting pagans and non-believers was probably more notable. There was also a significant economic benefit in the creation of new markets, the introduction of new products, the establishment of different trade routes and the bolstering of cultural exchange.

From the Muslim Arab viewpoint the crusades were a form of unprovoked aggression, raw western imperialism—a Christian 'Jihad' in a very real sense.

Again, the crusades added to the fear and mistrust previously encountered and manifested in the intrusions and expansions of the Islamic Empire. But this time it was the

Christian West that was seen as the instigator and aggressor. The crusades left a lasting impression on the Muslim mind. Even today, in 2006, the likes of Osama bin Laden in taped communications from who-knows-where refer to the west as 'crusaders', a term carrying a high degree of mockery and contempt.

The Ottoman Empire

The emergence of the Ottoman Empire was a consequence of the decline of the Byzantine and Mongol Empires. The latter, Khitans, Juchens and Tatars from the Mongolian plateau, reached their zenith in the 13th century under Genghis Khan and his sons and grandsons, Batu and Kubla Khan, a period when much of Asia and Asia Minor fell under their dominion. As these empires began to break up around the 14th century the empire of the Ottoman Turks took form. In 1299 a Turkish Muslim warrior by the name of Osman led a revolt against Christian Byzantine areas in Anatolia. The word 'Ottoman' is derived from Turkish for 'followers of Osman'.

By 1453 this movement had conquered Constantinople and built a vast and well-administered state. Constantinople is the only city in the world that straddles two continents. It was founded as Byzantium in the 7th century BC and was renamed Constantinople when the Roman Emperor, Constantine, moved the seat of the Roman Empire there in the 4th century. It was then renamed Istanbul by the Ottomans and, within a relatively short period of time, became a city twice the size of any European city, as well as an international center of power and culture. The Ottoman Turks created a formidable navy and dominated the Mediterranean Sea and Indian Ocean. In the

1500's it conquered Syria, Egypt, Morocco, Yemen, Persia and much of Hungary. It threatened the heart of Europe for two centuries and, on two occasions in history, reached the outskirts of Vienna before being turned back.

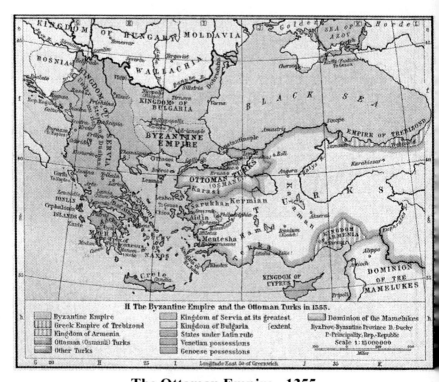

The Ottoman Empire - 1355
Courtesy of the University of Texas Libraries

The Ottoman Empire, 1481–1683.

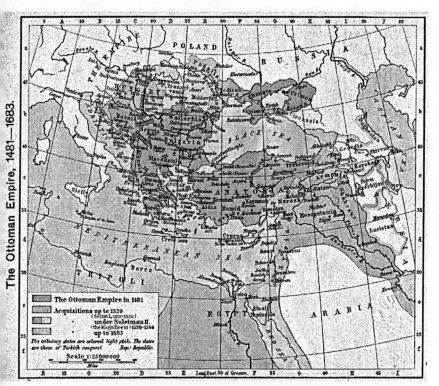

The Ottoman Empire - 15ᵗʰ Century
Courtesy of the University of Texas Libraries

Early Sultans felt they could gain little from the less advanced Europeans and saw no need to interface with them. An exception may have been in the field of the military when the superiority of western armaments was recognized and later emulated. Bernard Lewis in his book *The Middle East* noted that the Ottomans adopted western weapons out of military necessity and western uniforms out of cultural choice.

In contrast, travelers from the West often visited Ottoman cities to marvel at their advancement and to learn from their people. So although feared, the Ottomans were also admired, at least in their early years. At its peak this empire extended from the Balkans in Europe to Arabia and across North Africa. Its power and influence reached its zenith in the 16th century, the turning point being its naval defeat at Lepanto in 1571 by Venice and its allies, the Papal States and Spain.

The Ottoman Empire probably began an irreversible decline late in the 18th century when it came to be regarded as the 'sick man of Europe.' Mismanagement and austerity by the autocratic Sultan Abdul-Hamid led to the so-called 'revolt of the Young Turks', students and disgruntled military officers, who wanted not to reform the empire but somehow to return it to its former days of glory and greatness. Alas, that did not happen. John Esposito, in his book entitled *The Islamic Threat*, opines that some colonizers considered that as the balance of power and leadership shifted from the Muslim world to Europe, modernity was not just the result of conditions that produced the Enlightenment and the Industrial Revolution, but also of Christianity's inherent superiority as a religion and culture. The Christian world had overtaken the Muslim world as leaders of progress and development in virtually every field.

During the First World War, the Turks allied themselves with Germany and Austria-Hungary, a decision that proved to be the kiss of death for the weakened empire. After the war, at the Treaty of Sevres in 1920, the Ottomans were forced to grant independence to parts of its empire and to cede other parts of the Middle East to the administrative control of several European colonial powers, notably France and Britain.

The existence of the Ottoman Empire for over 400 years and its expansionist policies presented a constant threat to its neighbors, the Europeans in the west, the Russians in the north and the Asian countries to the east. So, once again, a substantial measure of fear, mistrust and antagonism was added to similar perceptions that had grown and was escalating between the peoples of Christian and other faiths and the Muslim world.

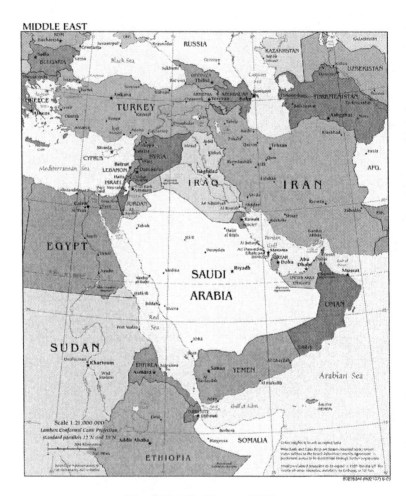

The Middle East - 2003
Courtesy of the University of Texas Libraries

European Colonialism in the Middle East

This period of western control and influence in the Middle East began primarily after World War I when the alliance of Germany, Austria-Hungary and Ottoman Empire were defeated. Separate peace agreements were signed with each of the warring factions, the effect of which was, among other things, to strip Germany of its colonies and to break up what remained of the Ottoman Empire, with parts mandated by the League of Nations to Britain and France. Under the Sykes-Picot Agreement of 1916 the Allied powers had basically arranged to divide and rule the Middle East region. At the Treaty of Sevres in 1920, the current day geopolitical map of the Middle East was decreed. Predominantly Christian Lebanon was carved out of Syria and both became colonies of the French, while most others, Iraq, Transjordan, Kuwait, etc. came under British control. Palestine was placed under joint Allied government jurisdiction and became a mandate of the League of Nations with its administration entrusted to Great Britain. The mandate concept was established under Article 22 of the Covenant of the League of Nations. It states, *"Certain communities formerly belonging to the Turkish Empire have reached a stage of development where their existence as independent nations can be provisionally recognized subject to the rendering of administrative advice and assistance by a Mandatory until such time as they are able to stand alone. The wishes of these communities must be a principal consideration in the selection of the Mandatory."*

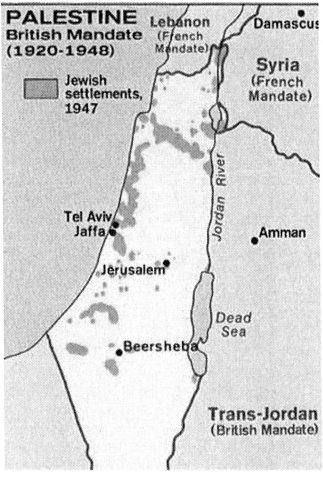

Palestine under the British Mandate
Courtesy of the University of Texas Libraries

The Hejaz, i.e. western Arabia, became a free and independent state. Iran, being outside the Ottoman Empire, was not addressed.

Professor John Esposito noted in his book, *The Islamic Threat*, that actions by Allied Powers after World War I reinforced the image of a militant west and created modern states whose artificial boundaries and appointed rulers had questionable political legitimacy. He also asserted that colonialism was experienced as a threat to Muslim identity and faith. As a result, belief in Christian superiority grew and educating the local populations in the ways and means of the West, as well as in Christian principles, was all part of an enlightened European plan to bring these people into the civilized 20th century.

During the World War I the local populations in the Middle East were encouraged to rise up against the Turks with the promise of support for their independence when the war was over. So revolt they did on the side of the Allies, and they were successful in creating considerable havoc on Turkish installations, disrupting supplies and assisting in a significant way in the defeat of the Turks in the Middle East. The exploits of T. E. Lawrence, better know as 'Lawrence of Arabia', in his role with the Arabs against their Turkish masters are amply romanticized. War came and was won, yet the dream of independence promised the Arabs by Britain did not materialize, creating another major disappointment and presenting another example of deceit which further eroded faith in the West and impeded any rebuilding of trust between the peoples of the region and their new masters.

The Rise of Zionism

Zionism can be characterized as a political movement for the creation of the national Jewish homeland for the Jewish people and the return of Jewish sovereignty to the land of their roots. The term "Zionism" was coined in 1893 by Nathan Birnbaum. In 1894 an Austrian author and journalist by the name of Theodor Herzl covered the famous and highly publicized treason trial of Alfred Dreyfus, an officer in the French army and a Jew, who had been falsely accused and convicted of spying for Germany. As he observed the trial unfold Herzl became convinced that Jews would never be treated equally and fairly outside of their own homeland. He began organizing those who sympathized with his views and developed strategies that would bring pressure on European powers to support a Jewish homeland. In 1897 at the First Zionist Congress in Basel, Switzerland, Herzl initiated the Zionist movement on a worldwide scale. Persecutions in Russia and events such as the Dreyfus Affair had convinced him and many others that Jews could not assimilate in a non-Jewish society, and the only remedy was to create an independent Jewish state. Thus the pronounced aim of Zionism was "to establish a home for Jewish people in Palestine, secured under public law." It is believed that Herzl was highly influenced by the 1862 teachings of the German Jewish socialist, Moses Hess, who rejected the notion of assimilation into European society, also believing that the solution to anti-Semitism was the creation of a national home for the Jews.

The Zionist Movement was a good deal more political than religious as it called for and encouraged the ingathering of all Jews into the Holy Land and the establishment of a political entity specifically for Jews. Certainly not all Jews have embraced the aims or the methods of the Zionists. In the early days and in order to allay fears of a major upheaval, the Zionists did not openly call for a national political state, but rather for a home within a nation where they could go and freely practice their religion and enjoy their own culture. Many Jews, and particularly many Orthodox Jews, point out that the Torah promises the return of the Jews to the Holy Land together with the Messiah, that it is to be a time of joy and peace. Regrettably, that is not the way Israel was established. One such group of Jewish dissidents called the Neturei Karte say the following on their web site.

"—We are opposed to the ideology of Zionism, a recent innovation, which seeks to force the end of exile. Our banishment from the Holy Land will end miraculously at a time when all mankind will unite in the brotherly service of the Creator."

This view may not be representative of mainstream Jewish public opinion, but perhaps it illustrates that the Zionist movement does not enjoy unanimous and unconditional support of all Jewish people.

Nevertheless, the Zionists proved themselves very resourceful and most effective in winning broad political and public support for their cause. It takes nothing away from their efforts but it is a fact that the support received from the various world powers for a Jewish homeland often had more to do with their own internal political interests than with a conviction that this was the right thing for the Jews or for the region. There were exceptions.

The creation of Israel enjoyed and, indeed, modern day Israel today enjoys a good deal of support from right wing protestant groups who believe that the establishment of Jews in Israel is a precondition for the second coming of Christ.

Britain's 'Balfour Declaration' in 1917 advocating a homeland for the Jews was heavily influenced by Britain's desire to obtain Jewish support for the war effort during WW I and its belief that a friendly state, beholden to Britain, would be an valuable asset in achieving its post-war Middle East policies.

According to President Harry Truman's memoirs, his immediate recognition of the state of Israel (exactly eleven minutes after receipt of Israel's declaration of independence!) was contrary to the advice and counsel of his State and Defense Departments but reflected his personal feeling that it would be possible to watch out for the long-range interests of the U.S. while at the same time helping the unfortunate victims of persecution find a home. He believed it was possible to implement the partition plan and still promote longer-range harmony and mutual benefits for both the Jews and the Arabs. And the Zionists were relentless in pursuit of their cause. In his memoirs President Truman noted that Jewish pressure on the White House did not diminish in the days following the partition vote in the U.N. In spite of this pressure the President remained faithful to his opinion that the proposed partition of Palestine could open the way for peaceful collaboration between the Arabs and the Jews.

Certainly not all Jews or Israelis are pleased with what Zionism has become today and Israeli policies in the West Bank and Gaza have not been universally embraced by all Jewish people. Prominent Israeli legislators and writers have spoken out vociferously against government actions in expanding settlements and suppressing Palestinian rights. Yet these moderate voices are silenced when violence is perpetrated on Jewish civilians.

The Balfour Declaration

An important milestone on the road to creation of a homeland for the Jews occurred in 1917. Anxious to obtain support for the war effort from the influential Jewish community, the British government issued the so-called Balfour Declaration, named after its foreign secretary, Lord Arthur James Balfour. This was a most significant development since it was the first time the Jews had been able to obtain anything like a real commitment for the establishment of a Jewish homeland. Aside from support for the war, His Majesty's Government was also planning its post-war Middle East strategy and the notion of a friendly state, beholden to Britain, was appealing, particular given the strategic location of Palestine near the Suez Canal. The declaration read:

"His Majesty's government views with favor the establishment in Palestine of a national home for the Jewish people, and will use its best endeavors to facilitate the achievement of this objective, it being clearly understood that nothing shall be done which may prejudice the civil and religious rights of the existing non-Jewish communities in Palestine, or the rights and political status enjoyed by Jews in other countries."

Lord Arthur James Balfour
British Foreign Secretary 1916-1919

This declaration was endorsed by the League of Nations in 1922 and became the basis for the later partition of Palestine that occurred after WW II. It is interesting to note that prior to finally settling on Palestine as the location for a Jewish homeland, serious offers were made to the Jews for lands in Uganda, and also in Argentina. Theodor Herzl, in fact, was in favor of the former, at least as an interim solution—"since it was available"—but this offer was rejected by the World Zionist Organization who held out for a place in the Holy Land where Jews had roots and history.

It is worth noting at the time of the Balfour Declaration in 1917, Jews owned but 3% of the land in Palestine and constituted less than 10% of the population, no more than about 56,000, half of who were recent immigrants escaping persecution in Russia.

It is also important to note that the caveat buried in this declaration, '—*it being clearly understood that nothing shall be done which may prejudice the civil or religious rights of the existing non-Jewish communities in Palestine*—' made implementation of the pledge, as worded, quite unachievable. It was virtually impossible that a homeland for Jews could be carved out of Palestine without in some way "prejudicing the civil and religious rights of the existing non-Jewish communities in Palestine." Britain no doubt began to fully and painfully realize that when it assumed its mandate role over Palestine in 1922.

The legal and moral basis by which Britain could make such a commitment, which in essence offered a people, dispersed in many countries outside the region, the land of a third country over which it had neither dominion nor rights, has always remained questionable by Arab and other governments. It was possibly rationalized simply as another imperialistic act considered common in those times.

Encouraged by the Balfour Declaration, Jewish immigration into Palestine accelerated in the years that followed. Many of the Jewish emigrants arriving in Palestine were genuinely surprised to find a settled population living there. They had heard that Palestine was, *"A land with no people for a people with no land."* Alas, there was a sizable Arab population long established in the land and the onslaught of newcomers understandably created a great deal of local tension and unrest between the incoming Jews, the local Arab inhabitants and the governing British. The immigrant Jews were seeking land and accommodations, and competing for jobs. Arab trust in the West hit a new low.

In May of 1939, yielding to Arab pressure, Britain, in its so-called White Paper terminated its commitment to Zionism and advocated instead the creation of a single Palestinian state within ten years. Jewish immigration was to be limited to 75,000 over the following five years with any further immigration subject to Arab consent. Needless to say this reversal did not go down well with the Jews. In May 1942 at the Biltmore Hotel in New York City, Zionist leaders demanded a Jewish state in all of western Palestine. The unfolding Holocaust in Germany added additional pressure to accommodate the fleeing victims and by 1944 the Irgun Zvai Leumi (National Military Organization), a guerrilla force led by Menachem Begin, who later became a prime minister of Israel, began an armed revolt against the restrictive immigration policies of the British in Palestine. By this time the Zionist movement and its aim for a homeland in Palestine had gained such momentum it was virtually impossible to slow down.

The Birth of Israel

During the time World War II was raging, or just after, several Arab states were granted independence; Lebanon in 1943, and Syria and Jordan in 1946, were among the few. Rulers of these states were hardly installed by a democratic process. They were pretty much appointed, set up and supported by the departing colonial powers who hoped to have secured a high degree of loyalty, dependence and future cooperation.

In November of 1947, the Balfour Declaration took concrete form with the decision by the United Nations to partition Palestine. Under UN Resolution 181, the Jewish state was to be awarded 56% of the land of Palestine with Jerusalem administered by a separate international body. At that time Jews owned or leased between 6 and 7 % of the land and constituted about 31% of the population.

Britain's contradictory commitments to the Arabs and the Jews, promising the former independence and the latter a homeland in Palestine, compromised its credibility with both parties. Arab objections to the Partition Plan were immediate but futile. In the voting for the U.N.'s partition resolution, all Middle Eastern countries together with Greece, Turkey, India, Pakistan, Afghanistan, and Cuba voted against the resolution. Those that voted in favor were most of the western powers, Canada, Australia, France and the U.S. and its allies in Europe and Latin America. Surprisingly, the USSR voted in favor of partition, purportedly to speed up British departure from the Middle East. It is interesting and perhaps foretelling that the United Kingdom, father of the Balfour Declaration and the Mandatory power in Palestine with no doubt the most intimate understanding of the dynamics on the ground there, abstained in the voting, together with China, Ethiopia, Yugoslavia and several Latin countries.

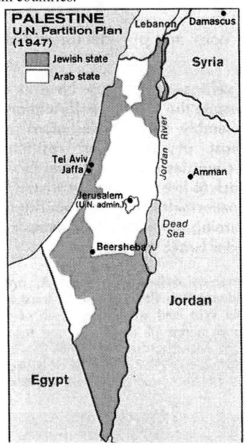

The U.N. Partition Plan - 1947
Courtesy of the University of Texas Libraries

The Arab delegation questioned the authority of the U.N. to make such a ruling and petitioned that the issue be submitted to the International Court of Justice for a judgment. The petition was denied and Arab outcries fell on deaf ears. Had the UN agreed to such a review and had the International Court of Justice upheld the authority of the United Nations in its decision, then perhaps the partition would have had more international legitimacy. Regrettably, that did not happen and the UN action, for all its intents and purposes, was viewed by the Arabs as another Western conspiracy against the Arab world, an act that has proved most difficult for Arab and many other countries of the world to willingly accept. It was viewed as a contravention of international law, a violation of the charter of the United Nations and unjust to the indigenous people of the region. The Arabs opposed partition because it made a mockery of Palestinian sovereignty; surrendered to non-resident immigrants the major portion of Palestinian land, which was not the UN's to give, and denied the local population its right of self-determination.

Understandably, the partition resolution heightened tensions in Palestine to an explosive point. The Arabs had from the beginning resisted, often violently, the massive immigration of Jews into Palestine. Between 1936 and 1939 they openly revolted against Britain's immigration policies and there were often violent confrontations between the local Arabs and the new Jewish settlers. Nevertheless, Jewish immigration continued to accelerate. One Palestinian historian asserts that between 1918 and 1946, the Jewish population in Palestine increased from 56,000 to 608,000, moving from 1/12 to 1/3 of the total population in just 28 years. Britain's efforts to impose limits to mitigate conflict with the Arabs raised the ire of Jewish extremists who intensified their own campaign of violent opposition to British policies.

Jewish immigrants who arrived in the 1920's and 1930's were quick to organize themselves and their communities. They set up labor unions, social organizations, and a security apparatus and organized their own militia, called the Haganah, which later proved itself an effective army against the Arabs. All these together laid the groundwork for a highly functional community that was able to quickly convert itself into workable governmental institutions when that opportunity arose.

To grow their numbers and to accommodate new comers, there were several obstacles that the Jews needed to overcome. First was the limit the British mandate placed on Jewish immigration. The bombing by Jewish extremists of the King David Hotel, where the British military was headquartered, was one clear message to Britain on its policy of limiting immigration. There were others. The second obstacle was basically the existence of a local population already settled and living on the land, and certain Jewish extremists began a campaign to encourage their departure—often by violent means. Unrest, frequent acts of violence and jockeying for position persisted throughout the winter of 1947-48 and into the spring. Finally, Britain concluded that administering the powder keg that Palestine was fast becoming was a rather hopeless, no-win situation that had no redeeming outcome. In May of 1948, Britain surrendered its mandate back to the United Nations. Regrettably, it had made little preparation for a successor administration to ensure law and order. In such an environment only chaos could prevail. The next day, May 14, 1948, the Jews declared the independence of the state of Israel. The parties to the conflict are not of one mind on whether Jewish advances beyond the boundaries allocated to them by the U.N. partition was unilateral or whether it was merely a reaction to the Arab resistance to the establishment of the Jewish state. Indeed, there are reports that a number of Arab towns and villages were in essence taken over in some way in the six months prior to the end of the British Mandate. Arab armies were mobilized to support the Palestinians, but they proved totally ineffective. The key difference between the Zionists and the Arabs was the former were united and determined, the latter divided and hesitant. According to some sources the Jews were outnumbered two to one yet were able to defeat the combined Arab armies. Some Palestinian historians, on the other hand, claim that the Arab armies were a poorly equipped token force of no more than 20,000 facing an organized and well-prepared Jewish armed force of 100,000. Whereas the United States denied arms shipments to both sides, the Israelis purported incurred some $500 million in military expenditures during the war, largely from Eastern Europe. The violence was intense and losses on both sides were extensive. According to Norman Finkelstein in his book, *The Holocaust Industry,* there were some 6000 Jewish casualties. Arab casualties were even higher. Following several ineffectual truces, and with the aid of Ralph Bunche of the United Nations, an armistice was finally arranged in early 1949. By that time the Jewish state had increased its size from the 56% of Palestine that had been allocated to it by the U.N. resolution to about 78%. In addition to the loss of the land, there were over 700,000 Arabs who fled their homes and became refugees in neighboring Jordan, Syria, and Lebanon. According to the Encarta Encyclopedia about half left out of fear and panic and the rest were forced out to make room for Jewish immigrants from Europe and from the Arab world.

According to UNRWA (the United Nations Relief and Works Agency) there were over 4.2 million refugees registered with it as of March 2005, of which about 1.1 million were still living in camps. 64% of Palestinian refugees are under the age of 30 with over 67,000 infants under the age of one.

The Armistice of 1949 did not put an end to the conflict between the newly established state of Israel and its neighbors. Between 1955 and 1992 there were some 65 United Nations resolutions condemning Israeli actions against the Palestinians or Arab states while, in that period, not one time were the Arabs condemned. That is not to say that the Arabs were totally innocent of abuses but Israel was less inclined to rely on the United Nations to air and redress complaints and tended to act directly and independently whenever it believed its interests were threatened. What is clear is that the war of 1948-49 put a new dimension on the Arab-Israeli conflict. The concept of the partition of Palestine, the initial issue, was supplanted by a new, more troubling and more ominous reality on the ground— a well organized, well armed and determined Jewish state with broad international recognition.

The Islamic Reawakening

Following the decline of the Islamic empire starting around the sixteenth century, history seemed unkind to the Islamic world. Not only had their great empire been broken apart, but also the balance of power, wealth, and enlightenment was shifting decisively to the West. Islamic revival varied from country to country and was generally a consequence of failed political, economic and social systems that had not maintained pace with the rest of the world. It was also disappointment with the positions of the West on a number of fronts such as, the Pakistan/Bangladesh War, the 1967 Arab/Israel conflict, and others. More than anything else it seemed a quest for greater, more significant recognition. For some it was an alternative to secularism, to nationalist aspirations, to capitalism and to communism. It offered a new identity based on the community of believers, the 'Umma', and common cultural and religious values. But the Islamic civilization remained somewhat isolated and inconsequential in the world arena. Some scholars have intimated that Islam is a singular civilization—persuaded of the superiority of its culture, yet preoccupied with the inferiority of its power. And failures were compounding.

The 1950s and 1960s were periods when Arab nationalism and socialism were on the rise. With such charismatic leaders as Jamal Abdel Nasser of Egypt, there grew hope that the Arab countries might be able to put aside their differences and unite into a single, powerful Arab nation and stand united on common issues and against foreign intrusions. But Abdel Nasser's renegade policies and independent aspirations were soon perceived as a threat to Western interests. When the United States reneged on a promise to help finance the Aswan Dam on the Nile River, Abdel Nasser reacted by nationalizing the Suez Canal, an action that led to the coordinated attack on Egypt by Israel, Britain and France in 1956. The geographic gains in that brief war were quickly reversed with pressure from President Eisenhower of the United States. Notwithstanding the Islamic aversion to communism, Abdel Nasser opened Egypt's doors to Soviet aid and military assistance in defiance of America's reluctance to provide such support. He went further and forged a political merger with Syria in 1958. Called the United Arab Republic, the UAR was a first step in what many in the area hoped would begin a unification of the Arab world. Alas, this initiative lasted a mere three years. However, Abdel Nasser's brand of socialism prevailed in much of the so-called non-aligned world and became, in essence, an alternative to both capitalism and communism. It advocated a new social order based on state planning and control of major industries and financial institutions, and, most importantly, independence from both super powers. Among Arabs, it promoted resistance to all forms of colonialism, personified in the creation of the Jewish State of Israel on Arab land in the midst of the Islamic world. While Arab nationalism was primarily secular in nature it did recognize and ensure a place for an Islamic component in Arab identity and culture. By and large, Arab countries shared a common language, a common history and a common religion. Perhaps predictably, in a relatively short time the differences in Arab views, economic disparity, conflicting goals and parochial interests proved too much. Thus ended an experiment with Arab nationalism that has since been unable to find renewal.

The six-day war in 1967 was another significant blow to the Arab and Islamic dream of a reawakening and a new beginning. The Arab regimes, principally Egypt, Syria, and Iraq, were bristling under the weight of the growing power of Israel and the inability of the Arabs to secure their own political and economic destinies. Their saber rattling exemplified by the boycott of the Straits of Tiran to Israel shipping, the massing of Egyptian troops on the border, Egypt's request to the United Nations to remove its 'peacekeepers' from the area and other provocations gave Israel all the reasons it felt needed to initiate war on its neighbors. Several scholars and active participants have suggested that these provocative actions by the Arabs were themselves deliberately provoked by Israeli aggressions in disputed territories and against the Syrian air force. The implication is that these Israeli actions were part of a greater, well-designed strategy to induce a war, for which Israel was ready, to achieve additional territorial gains. Within two days of the beginning of the war the air forces of both Syria and Egypt were obliterated and in six days Israel had managed to defeat the Arab armies and to occupy the Syrian Golan Heights, the Egyptian Sinai Peninsula, the Jordanian West Bank and East Jerusalem. Four cease-fires were ordered by the Security Council but the fighting only stopped after Israel had secured its control of East Jerusalem. The war not only lost more Arab lands to Israel, but also created another 400,000 Arab refugees. According to several Arab historians the number of Arab refugees displaced in the 1948 and 1967 wars exceeded 1.8 million. Others have estimated the number as low as 1.1 million. Norman Finkelstein, in his book, observed that after the Israeli stunning victory in the 1967 war, the US moved to incorporate Israel as a strategic asset, the objective being to defend US interest in the region against the Arab masses. The six-day War revealed the full extent of Arab military, economic and political weakness.

There was a measure of pride restored when, in 1973, President Anwar Sadat of Egypt managed to surprise Israel and regain a part of the Sinai Peninsula it had lost in the 1967 Six-day War. It was only the massive supply of US military equipment and material from Europe that forestalled an even greater victory for the Arabs. It was also a costly war for the Arabs as, altogether, there was significant loss of life. Although the war ended with something of a stalemate, it was hailed as a great victory by the Arabs. The Israelis also hailed it as something of a victory, but soon after, Prime Minister Golda Meir and her Minister of Defense, Moshe Dayan, both stepped down and the entire Sinai was returned to Egyptian sovereignty a few years later. This war again demonstrated, in no uncertain terms, the full extent of America's dedication and commitment to Israel. Most significantly, it triggered the first ever use of oil as a weapon. In a rare show of unity, the Arab oil producing states applied a boycott of Arab oil to the United States and to those countries that facilitated America's intervention that thwarted Arab advances. The boycott resulted in significant, worldwide economic hardships and spurred concerted efforts to conserve energy and to reduce reliance on Middle Eastern oil.

A greater Islamic victory was finally perceived to have occurred in Iran in 1979. Shah Mohammad Reza Pahlavi had been reinstalled on the Peacock Throne in 1953 through a CIA-led ouster of Prime Minister Mohammad Mossadeqh, a fiery anti western nationalist who had overthrown the young Shah and had taken steps to expropriate the oil industry which was largely in the hands of British oil companies. The United States supported the re-installed Shah politically and economically, and trained and equipped his military. Thus, Iran became a staunch ally of the West, particularly of the US, and a credible buffer between the Soviets to the north and the rich oilfields of the Middle East to the south. Although the Shah introduced many reforms in Iran, he ruled very much as a dictator and failed to recognize or to deal decisively with growing internal discontent. The Shah was effectively overthrown by the rising tide of religious fervor personified in the exiled Ayatollah Ruhollah Khomeini who returned triumphant to accept the mantle of supreme leader of the Shiite faith as well as the head of the newly proclaimed Islamic Republic of Iran. (Whereas in Islam there is no hierarchy as such, it is interesting to note how the structure of the Islamic Republic of Iran was set up. Bernard Lewis called it an institutional 'Christianization of Islam' with the Ayatollah Khomeini in a position much like the Pope of Christendom, a college of 'Cardinals', a bench of 'Bishops' and an 'inquisition'.) There is a view that the upheaval in Iran may have been less a religiously motivated struggle and more a popular uprising against a brutal dictator who had sold his soul and country to the West. Iranians were united more by their opposition to the Shah's autocratic regime than by any shared theology. In any event, the ouster of the Shah was hailed as a marvelous Islamic victory, which reverberated throughout the Islamic world. It was hailed as an example of the resurgence of Islamic power, pride and influence—a veritable triumph over the West. The Islamic revolution stimulated an Islamic revival far beyond the borders of Iran, spilling over into Arab and other Muslim countries, even to those countries that were not particularly sympathetic to the Iranian political entity or its

Shiite form of Islam. It was a validation of Islam as still a potent force to be reckoned with, a true revival and reawakening not seen since the early days of Islamic conquest. However, it did little to stimulate political unity. Its effects were primarily confined to the faith, the Koran and the teachings and interpretations of the Prophet Mohammad and the belief that Islam was an all encompassing and self-propelling force. With this came disdain, even hatred, for western culture, which was perceived as corrupting their religious values, and for super power intervention and their apparent designs on Iranian resources.

The 1990 Gulf War was yet another event in the history of the turbulent Middle East that again demonstrated what the Arabs considered to be the double standard of the West. Although most Arab nations were highly critical of Saddam Hussein's policies and, particularly, of his invasion of Kuwait—and more than a few joined in the Western coalition against him—they were equally dismayed that the West considered Iraq's offenses against its Arab neighbor greater than those of Israel against its Arab neighbors. Indeed, in 2003, the U.S. and Britain again waged war against Iraq purportedly for its failure to respect UN resolutions and to destroy, or at least reveal, its weapons of mass destruction. Arab countries were baffled at the importance placed on the ignored UN resolutions when there are also many such resolutions that other countries continue to ignore with impunity. This reality did nothing to strengthen Arab confidence in the West or to trust it to pursue an even-handed policy in the Middle East.

The Islamic revival was by no means a marginal happening. It was totally mainstream and pervasive, permeating the very depths of Islamic society. It stimulated a true examination of the Islamic being in all its facets. But it also created something of a dilemma. Was this revival to take the shape of a restoration or a reformation? There are several aspects of Islam that are important to note as we attempt to understand. In Islam there is no Pope, no one supreme leader, and no one spokesperson. Adherents are free to express their own views that may or may not be accepted universally across the faith, and, indeed, often strong differences arise. A mosque is like a church in that it is a place of worship but, unlike a church, a mosque is not an institution. In general, there is no one Islamic political agenda or position. Each sect of Islam, each Islamic country, even each mosque often takes positions pretty much independent of the other. They tend to be anti-foreign, but not anti-progress. They tend to be well organized and highly disciplined. Contrary to what many in the West believe violence is not a common Muslim characteristic. Adherents of Islam often have a stronger affinity to Muslims in other countries than loyalty to their own state. There are elements of Islam that call for a return to the days and the practices of the early Islamists. They advocate a reversion to the values and literal teachings of the Prophet and his early followers. There are others who interpreted this revival as a call to reform Islam, maintaining its character but adapting to the changes of today's age. The battle between the restorers and the reformers continues. Both struggle with modernity believing it is possible to modernize without westernizing. One of the conflicts between the West and the East is simply this. Often, the West tends to believe that in order to modernize one must become like the West in its values, its culture, and its social, judicial and legislative systems. By and large, the Islamic East rejects this notion, choosing to believe it can modernize and thrive totally within the context of its own Islamic culture and values. The argument certainly has both merit and logic.

Countries in the Middle East have experimented with secularism, with socialism and with nationalism, all pretty much unsuccessfully. Muslims do tend to condemn westernism and secularism, but not modernization, as such. Advanced, even leading edge, technology and development are accepted, but everything must be made compatible with, and subordinated to, the teachings of Islam. Muslims have long considered their religion as self sufficient and all inclusive.

The West has tried to understand Islam in the context of its own Christian culture that places beliefs strictly in the personal or private arena, rather than in a broader context of a total, self-sufficient and shared way of life. Regrettably, at times in history, Muslims, as have Christians and Jews, used religion to justify wars, violence and persecutions. Such acts tend to emanate from the radical fringes rather than from the silent mainstream. Indeed, in several countries Muslim groups have been driven to violent acts because they were explicitly precluded from participating in the democratic process and denied legitimate gains in the ballot box. Fareed Zakaria, in his book, *The Future of Freedom*, asserts that this denial of participation in the democratic process and the absence of basic liberties are the primary ingredients in the growth of terrorism in the Arab world. Examples can be cited from 20th century Algeria, Egypt, Turkey and Tunisia. John Esposito noted that to equate Islam and Islamic fundamentalism with extremism is to judge Islam only by those who wreak havoc.

Islam is a faith, a moral code, a set of laws, a judicial system, and a form of government. Muslims believe nothing else is needed. The debate continues.

Meanwhile the West tends to view Islam as backward and radical. The East in turn views the Christian West as arrogant, intrusive and morally corrupt. Benjamin Barber, in his book entitled *Jihad Versus McWorld*, he says, "President Bush was speaking to the world at large when he said, 'You are with us or you are with the terrorists.'...It is not that the world must join America: McWorld already operates on this premise and the premise is precisely the problem. Rather, America must join the world on whatever terms it can negotiate, on an equal footing with the world. Whether a product of arrogance or prudence, the demand that the world join the United States simply cannot secure results. It defies the very interdependence to which it is addressed. It assumes a sovereign autonomy that the US does not and cannot enjoy."

Several historians have tried to define the conflict between Islam and the West as a genuine clash of civilizations. They tend to agree that efforts of the West to universalize its values and institutions, to maintain a worldwide military presence, to parade its economic superiority and to intervene in foreign adventures does nothing to promote harmony and appreciation among its Muslims neighbors. Between 1980 and 1995, for example, it has been reported that there were 17 Western military operations in the Arab Middle East, and between 1757 to 1919 there were ninety-two acquisitions of Muslim territories by non-Muslim governments, and only sixty-nine of these were back in Muslim hands by 1995.

Muslims are fiercely anti communist. The Islamic faith is probably more incompatible with communism than it is with capitalism. When communism self-destructed in the late 1980's, a common enemy was removed and the West and the Islamic world were then left facing one another, each now the perceived major threat of the other.

Impressive Israel

Modern day Israel was established in 1948 following the 1947 United Nation's Resolution 181 that decreed partition of Palestine and the War between the Jews and the Arabs that followed. While the UN had earmarked for Israel 56% of the land area of Palestine, when the war ended Israel constituted about 78 % of the former Palestine.

Map courtesy of the University of Texas Library

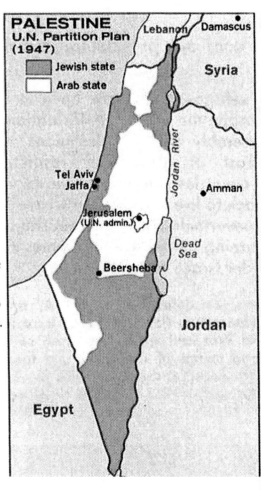

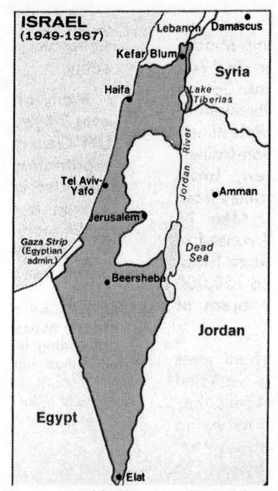

Map courtesy of the University of Texas Libraries

Since the 1967 war Israel has occupied the rest of what was Palestine plus the Syrian territory of the Golan Heights. Until 1979, after the peace treaty with Egypt was concluded, Israel also occupied the whole of the Sinai Peninsula.

Israel & the Occupied Territories after June 1967
Courtesy of the University of Texas Libraries

In August 2005 Israel took the unilateral decision to withdraw its settlements and military forces from the Gaza Strip, returning it to the jurisdiction of the Palestinian

Authority. This withdrawal, while an essential step in achieving long term peace, is not the end of the story nor has it resulted in a totally independent and self sustaining political entity for Gaza. There remain many practical issues to be resolved. Control of the border crossings, access to the West Bank, the opening of an airport and shipping ports and basic security are but a few of the crucial matters that require resolution. Moreover and most importantly, the Palestinians must demonstrate they can indeed govern responsibly and efficiently. As of this writing, just after the elections of January 25, 2006, the signs are not encouraging. Hamas, the victor in these elections, has not advanced a program or policy statement that inspires confidence it can advance stability, credibility and acceptability.

The Encarta Encyclopedia estimates the population of Israel in 2002 at approximately six million, of which some 18% are Arab, mostly Muslim. Interestingly, this estimate includes the Golan Heights and East Jerusalem, which, in the eyes of most of the world, are still 'Arab occupied areas.' About half of the population of Israel lives in the three major metropolitan centers of Tel Aviv-Yafo, Jerusalem and Haifa. Nearly 1/3 of world Jewry lives in Israel. For the most part Jews in Israel are immigrants or descendants of immigrants. As of 1997 38% of the total Jewish population had been born outside Israel, coming from over 100 different countries. All Jews are welcome in Israel and citizenship for them is pretty much automatic; not true for any other ethnic or national group. There are two main groupings of Jews. The Ashkenazim, originating mainly in Germany and from Central and Eastern Europe, tend to be the more influential and generally more involved in government. The Sephardim, originating mainly from Spain, North Africa and the Middle East, are generally less affluent and less politically active.

Israel has no formal written constitution, but its legislature passes so-called basic laws from time to time that guide government operations and activities. The ultimate authority in Israeli governance is the Knesset, a legislative parliament of 120 members selected for four-year terms on the bases of political party election results. Israel is a country of many political parties and in its history it has been most difficult for one party to rule except in coalition with one or more other parties. Decisions and policies are therefore often compromises necessary to maintain power.

Since independence in 1948, Israel has made great strides in many fields. Jewish immigrants brought with them from their birthplaces skills, knowledge and experience. These assets together with massive aid, principally from the United States and from Jewish communities overseas, combined with inexpensive Arab labor provided an impressive structural framework and an effective engine of growth. They drained swamps, irrigated deserts and drilled water wells. They encouraged education by building universities and scientific and cultural institutions. They developed a manufacturing base and promoted tourism.

But independence and prosperity has not brought security to Israelis. Whereas they have developed an effective brand of democracy and enjoy one of the highest per capita incomes in the world, they have been unsuccessful in reaching an accommodation with their neighbors who continue to harbor open hostility. Many Arabs continue to view the imposition of Israel in their midst as illegal and unjust, and some openly reject its presence in any form. However, for most other Arabs the only injustice that needs correction now is the occupation of the West Bank and the Golan Heights that were seized during the 1967 war, and the issue of the Palestinian refugees. Israel's attention and resources are split between the economic and social needs of its own people and the need to suppress resistance from Arabs in the occupied territories. Israel is virtually the only country in the world today that has persisted in the occupation of land that is not theirs and imposes a military regime over its people. The rejection of the Arabs of this state of affairs continues to negatively impact the security of the Israelis and the stability of the region. As the conflict continues to fester and as more blood is spilled, public opinion in the area and beyond is becoming more polarized and a lasting, mutually satisfactory solution more difficult to envision.

Ariel Sharon has left a lasting imprint on Israel and the Palestinian issue. In his early days he was a brilliant military commander, but always a maverick who followed his own instincts. His adventure into Lebanon in 1982 against the orders of his superiors was only one such example. His alleged complicity in the Sabra and Shatila massacres in Lebanon in 1982, which was perpetrated by a Christian militia, would have led to the eclipse of most people, but not Sharon who bounced back with vigor. Ironically, in his early unwavering encouragement and support for settlement expansion he created for himself one of his most serious obstacles when, as Prime Minister, he recognized their impediment to peace. His relentless pursuit of those committing acts of terror on Israelis earned him broad admiration and a loyal following in Israel— and the hostility of the Palestinians. His willingness to make tough decisions, to take on unpopular causes, and to risk and to endue wrath within his own party and his closest allies are examples of his determination and persistence. The world will never know if his continued leadership would have led to an enduring peace or to greater turmoil.

Influential Iraq

No treatise on the Middle East conflict would be complete without including Iraq. Mesopotamia, Babylon, Iraq, whatever the name, has been at the center of power and conflict throughout its long history. Ancient civilizations going back over 3000 years flourished along the banks of the Tigris and Euphrates Rivers. After the name 'Israel', Iraq by its various names is the most numerous in the Bible. The Assyrians, Babylonians, Chaldeans and Sumerians all, at one time or another, have occupied and ruled this land. It was conquered by the Persians in 500 BC and then taken by Alexander the Great in 331 BC. In 115 AD it became a part of the Roman Empire that lasted for about 500 years. In 637 AD it was overrun by the Arabs who introduced the Arabic language and converted the inhabitants to Islam. From 750 AD to 1250 under the Abbasid dynasty, Baghdad was the capital of the Islamic Empire, its wealth and advances in science, agriculture, mathematics and many other fields renown throughout the civilized world. The Mongols invaded Iraq in the 1200s, the Ottoman Turks in 1534. After World War I Iraq was made a British mandate, achieving quasi independence from Britain in 1932. In 1958 the Hashemite King that had been installed by the British following World War II was brutally assassinated and his government overthrown by a military junta, followed eventually by none other than Saddam Hussein, one of the principal instigators.

Iraq is a large country, some 168,000 square miles in area, 5% larger than California, 78% larger than Great Britain, 20% smaller than France. Its population approaches 25 million inhabitants of whom 15% are Sunni Kurds and 80% Arab Sunni and Shiite. Although the majority of the population is Shiite, all rulers in this century have been Sunni Muslim. So there are three major but distinct 'ethno-religious' groupings in Iraq today that aspire to some form of autonomy and hence complicating the creation of a unified, widely supported political entity. There are the Kurds in the North, the Arab Shiites largely in the south and the Arab Sunnis mainly in the middle. In the Arab world the Iraqis have tended to be among the most progressive and advanced. However, under the dictatorships of the last 45 years, progress has been stifled. Iraq has been further weakened by the long and destructive Iraq-Iran war, which lasted some eight years, by the Gulf war in 1991, occasioned by the Iraqi invasion of Kuwait, then by twelve years of UN sanctions which followed that war, and finally by the US and British led "Operation Iraqi Freedom" in 2003, a war waged initially to find and destroy Iraqi 'weapons of mass destruction' (WMD), later to topple the repressive regime of Saddam Hussein and to restore freedom and democracy to the Iraqi people.

Iraq is a country rich in human resources as well as natural resources, including water, a scarce commodity in the Middle East. Some 9-10% of the world's known proven petroleum reserves lie within the borders of Iraq. These attributes, together with its strategic position in the Middle East, thrust upon Iraq a key role in Arab and regional political matters.

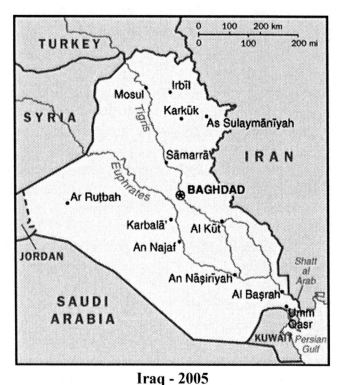

Iraq - 2005
Courtesy of the University of Texas Libraries

Saddam Hussein formally took over power in 1979, but was influential politically long before that. When he waged war on Iran in the early 1980s, the US supplied Iraq considerable intelligence as well as military and financial aid. He was fighting a common enemy and, therefore, at least for a period of time, he was treated as an ally. That relationship reversed itself in the run up to the invasion of Kuwait and the first Gulf war. The world vigorously debated the 2003 war against Iraq to remove Saddam from power and to ensure complete elimination of his weapons of mass destruction, assuming indeed that he still retained such weaponry. It was demanded that he prove to the international community that Iraq no longer has such fearsome weapons. Indeed, most observers seemed convinced that Saddam was concealing at least some part of his weapons program. Apart from the dilemma of how one goes about proving that he does not have something, one might surmise that with sophisticated satellite surveillance systems, covert operators and years of UN inspections, the reality of Iraqi weapons capability would have been reasonably well nailed down.

The action eventually taken against Iraq by the United States and its "coalition of the willing" became a divisive issue within the United Nations, with Germany and France, together with Russia and China, having insisted that evidence of a direct linkage between Iraq and the world's terrorist organizations first be established, and that the UN inspectors be given more time to seek out all illegal arms that threaten peace and stability.

During his rule Saddam had not endeared himself to many. He was feared for the strength of his army, his personal ruthlessness and his unpredictability. On the other hand, he was admired by the many who felt victimized by the West. He was an Arab Muslim leader who had successfully defied the West and resisted their combined military might. He managed somehow to parley clear defeats into marvelous victories, at least in the eyes of his own people. He had also proven himself an adept survivor, which is probably the main reason his Arab neighbors were loathed to antagonize him. There seems to be widespread consensus that stability in the region will be secured with different, more enlightened and benevolent leadership in Iraq. As of this writing, April 2006, the ability of the new Iraqi leadership elected in December 2005 to restore security and unify the three main, very vocal and independent-minded, ethnic or religious groupings that constitute the Iraqi population, is yet to be proven. Meanwhile, the coalition troops and the Iraqi forces they are training daily encounter violent protests and armed resistance by disenchanted Iraqis, mainly Sunni, retaliating against the loss of their privileged position enjoyed under the Baathist regime. Exacerbating the situation further, a significant influx of Muslim fighters from other countries has converged on Iraq to wage a clandestine war against foreign military presence in a Muslim country and no doubt other grievances against the West. It has been estimated that as many as 75 such groups may exist, most operating on their own agenda and owing allegiance to no one in particular. Not all Iraqis seem convinced that a foreign power, regardless of how benevolent, is preferable to an Iraqi autocrat. Many now reason that under Saddam's regime, though repressive, at least they had jobs and a living wage, they had reliable electricity, water and medical service and they did not fear for their lives on the streets of Baghdad.

The preoccupation of the Bush Administration with Saddam's overthrow, pretty much to the exclusion of other equally or even possibly more menacing international threats, such as the North Korea nuclear crisis and the Israeli-Palestinian conflict, has been hard for many in the area to fathom. Failure to comply with UN resolutions, often cited as a reason for war, smacks as a double standard when there are other countries, some close allies of the United States, who have ignored UN resolutions for years with impunity. To date meaningful links to Al Qaeda and other terrorist groups have been unconvincing and inconclusive, and Iraq's threat to unleash weapons of mass destruction on the world seems to have been based more on speculation than on fact. Nevertheless, few countries would disagree that the world, and most certainly the region, is better off absent the Saddam Iraqi regime, assuming that some sense of cohesion in Iraq can be restored. Even Saddam's Arab neighbors and erstwhile supporters are no doubt relieved that the threat he posed to regional stability has been lifted. But history will continue to question whether the hard facts at hand justified a preemptive war with all the inherent peril involved, the human loss and widespread destruction in Iraq, the enormous costs to the United States and its coalition partners, the negative impact on the worlds' economies, the weakening of the United Nations and the adverse reaction it is evoking from the Islamic world. Saddam's Iraq was a 'problem' for the region, but the Palestinian-Israeli conflict is now, and continues to be, a major 'disaster'. Yet it has remained curiously sidelined for too many years—with fears and mistrust between the Muslim East and the Christian West growing, and divisions deepening in a defining conflict which grows more and more polarized.

Although the war toppling the Saddam regime proved to be short, insurgency, instability and anxiety persist to this day. These are circumstances when an effective United Nations involvement is most needed. Whereas it was not an active participant in the decision to make war, the UN must nevertheless play a key role in building the peace. This must remain one of its all-important provinces in the pursuit of world harmony and tranquility. Its active involvement in ensuring fair and open Iraqi elections was most effective and added credibility and acceptability to the process. Now more intense participation is called for.

The constitution drafted by the Iraqi government which was elected in January 2005 was accepted by the people in a referendum in October 2005. However, espousal and commitment by the Sunni Arabs will require certain amendments to that constitution. This will be an important test for the newly elected, Shiite-led government. If this Iraq experiment with democracy is indeed successful and if there results a sustained democratic chain reaction throughout the Middle East, as the Bush Administration predicts, then, clearly, war may have been justified. But, at the same time, a new and potentially dangerous precedent may have been set, a precedent that legitimizes preemptive attacks on regimes, however bad they may be, that may not really pose a clear and definitive threat to the international community. Will history record this latest Iraqi war as an insightful decision or an exacerbation of an already precarious relationship with the Islamic world?

Inaccessible Iran

Iran can trace its history back to around 1200 B.C. when the Elamites ruled what is now southern Iran. In the following 500-600 years two related peoples from the northern kingdoms of Russia and Central Asia migrated south establishing the Kingdom of Media in the north and occupying the area to the south which was later named Persis by the Greeks, and from which the name Persia is derived. The Assyrians plundered parts of the area in 640 B.C. and occupied both kingdoms until the Medes managed to wrestle from them control of the entire area in the 600's. The Persians remained under the rule of the Medes until about 550 B.C. when Cyrus the Great revolted and overthrew their Median masters. Under Cyrus the Great, Persia expanded its dominion to include Babylon, Syria and Palestine. Under Darius, in about 500 B.C., Persia reached its territorial zenith extending its borders eastward to India and westward as far as Greece. Darius established a strong central government, building roads and irrigation projects and coining money. After Darius' reign the empire began to falter. In 330 B.C. Alexander the Great conquered all of Iran, and his successors ruled for over 80 years. Later invaders included the Romans and the Sassanids. In 641 A.D. an Arabian Army invaded Iran and ruled for about 200 years, imposing Islam as the chief religion, displacing Zoroastrian, and introducing the Arabic alphabet. Iran soon flourished, becoming a center of art, literature and science. The Muslim Empire began to weaken around the edges in the 800's and Iran broke up into smaller kingdoms, soon falling prey to the Seljuk Turks from Turkistan, then the Mongols. Under the feared Mongol, Genghis Khan, the country was ravaged, entire cities destroyed and monuments and works of art lost. In the 1500's internal disputes among the Mongols opened the way to the emergence of the Iranian Safavid dynasty. Iran was ruled briefly by Afghanistan between 1722 and 1736, until it was freed by Nadir Shah, the last of the great Persian conquerors.

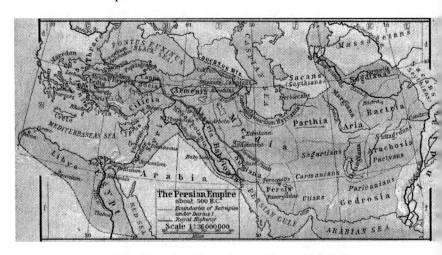

The Persian Empire – Circa 500 BC
Courtesy of the University of Texas Libraries

During the late 1800's and early 1900's Iran came under the influence, and sometimes direct control, of the Russians and the British, the former to gain access to warm water ports in the

Persian Gulf, the latter to protect India from Napoleon's advances. Wary of continued foreign designs on their country and concerned about government corruption and indifference, the Iranian people, in 1905, forced the government to adopt a constitution and to elect a parliament, regrettably abandoned some years later.

Iran became a battleground in World War I even though it had declared itself neutral. The oilfields in Baku on the Caspian Sea and those in southern Iran had already been identified as strategic assets, to be secured by the combatants at all costs.

Modern Iran began under the leadership of Reza Shah Pahlavi when he seized power in 1921. As Shah (i.e. king) he began to liberate the country from foreign influence, to modernize institutions, to set up an efficient government and a legal system based on French law, and to build infrastructure, schools and hospitals.

The Shah tried to maintain a neutral role for Iran in World War II but its oil resources again were too vital and too tempting to be left alone in war time. Both Britain and Russia invaded Iran in 1941, forcing the Shah to abdicate in favor of his son, Mohammad, who signed a treaty with both Britain and Russia. The treaty provided that Britain retained control of the lucrative oil resources in the south.

The late 1940's and 1950's were periods of great political and social unrest in Iran. Under the fiery socialist Prime Minister, Mohammad Mossadegh, the oil fields were nationalized and both the Shah and the British ousted. In a CIA instigated revolt in 1953, the Prime Minister was himself overthrown, the Shah restored to power and the oilfields returned to the British, albeit this time with American participation as compensation for its direct support in the ouster of Mossadegh.

Under Shah Mohammad Pahlavi, many reforms were introduced but these were primarily in the financial and industrial sectors. Social programs and other basic concerns of the people were largely ignored, rights were curtailed and a very authoritarian and intolerant form of government evolved. The Shah was increasingly seen as a tool of the West, who was imposing western values and practices that were viewed as violations of Islamic tradition. His policies even antagonized the more western educated class who resented their exclusion from participation in the future of their country.

One voice of dissent, that of the charismatic Ayatollah Ruhollah Khomeini, emerged as powerful and most pervasive. Khomeini was a respected cleric with a wide following, created and maintained through an extensive network of students. His growing significance eventually earned him exile, first to Iraq and later to France. But Khomeini's influence and appeal only broadened with his departure. Demonstrations by his followers and the rioting which ensued were suppressed with deadly force, creating martyrs whose burials stimulated more demonstrations and new martyrs in an escalation that rapidly spread throughout the country. Recognizing his loss of control and suffering from a debilitating cancer, the Shah finally departed the country on January 1979, never again to return. Two weeks later, amid jubilation and celebration, the Ayatollah returned to Iran to establish the Islamic Republic of Iran, with himself as the de facto head of state and chief arbiter.

Iranian-U.S. relations continued to deteriorate until, finally, on November 4, 1979, with resentment over the Shah's admittance into the United States for medical treatment, the American Embassy in Tehran was seized by a rebellious mob and the embassy staff of some 60 members held hostage. Sanctions and the freezing of Iranian assets in the United States did not produce a settlement to the crisis. It was only after Iran found itself at war with Iraq that they were prepared to agree to release the hostages, exactly 444 days after their capture.

The Islamic Republic of Iran - 2005
Courtesy of the University of Texas Libraries

In 1980, fearing that the ascendancy of a Shiite republic in Iran would foment unrest among his own Shiite majority in Iraq and sensing that a weakened and disorganized Iran would enable him to retake full control of the strategic and often disputed Shatt-al-Arab waterway that separates the two countries and maybe even the oil fields in Iran's western region of Khuzestan, Saddam Hussein invaded Iran. The war raged for 8 years, by some estimates claiming over a million and a half lives, debilitating both countries but ending in something of a stale mate.

Iran shared with Iraq and North Korea the dubious distinction of being on President George W. Bush's "Axis of Evil" list, a label purportedly earned for its support of terrorist organizations around the world and for its reluctance to adhere to international protocols. Its defiance of the International Atomic Energy Commission and its apparent quest to obtain a nuclear weapon capability has continued to heighten concerns in the West.

As of this date, despite a few earlier signs of reform, the government remains effectively in the grips of the senior religious establishment. Nevertheless, there appears to be a latent, perhaps sizable, grass roots reform sentiment in the country and an interest in renewal of international relationships. The recent election to the presidency of the conservative Mayor of Tehran, Mahmoud Ahmadinejad, was seen as a clear setback for the progressive movement. His apparent insistence on developing a nuclear weapons capability, in spite of his denials of that aim, is indeed ominous.

Iran remains and is destined to continue to be a significant player in the regional arena. Its sheer size, 13% larger than the land mass of Great Britain, France, Germany and Italy combined, coupled with a large and growing population of close to 70 million, and sitting on 9-10% of the world's known oil resources makes it a presence that cannot be ignored nor taken for granted.

Seasoned Syria

Damascus, or Dimashq or, in Arabic, 'Sham' is the capital of Syria and claims to be the oldest, continuously occupied city in the world. Certainly it has often played a central role in ancient times, in Biblical times and in the current turmoil in the Middle East.

The first know settlers in what is now Syria probably were Semites migrating from the Arabia peninsula around about 3500 B.C., although there is evidence of unidentified peoples in northern Syria before that time. In those early times independent city-states rose up in various parts of the land, some of which developed sophisticated civilizations. Among them were the Akkadians, the Canaanites, the Amorites, the Arameans, and the Phoenicians. The latter settled mainly along the coast and became a seafaring city-state, extending their influence throughout the Mediterranean area. The Hebrews (Jews) entered Syria during the late 1200's B.C. The Assyrians conquered most of Syria in 732 B.C. and ruled until the Chaldeans took over in 572 B.C. Following this, the Persians successfully invaded Syria until they in turn were defeated at the hands of Alexander the Great. The Seleucids brought Greek culture with their rule which succumbed to the invasion of the Romans in 64 B.C., a rule which endured in one form or another for some 700 years. In 636 A.D. Syria fell to the invading

Muslim armies who converted most of the country to the Islamic religion. Damascus became the capital and principal city of the Islamic Empire from 661 to 750 AD.

The Ottomans entered Syria in 1516 and ruled until the end of World War I in 1918. Under the terms of the Treaty of Sevres in 1920, Syria and a host of other Middle Eastern countries were placed under the mandate of either Britain or France. Syria and Lebanon were assigned to the French to administer until they were deemed ready for independence. Lebanon, once considered by some a part of Syria, was carved out of it and rendered a separate, largely Christian entity. During WW I Britain encouraged the Arabs to revolt against the Ottoman Turks, who had allied themselves with the German/Italian Axis, in return for which they promised support for Arab independence. Indeed, the resistance of Syria and other Arab countries succeeded in accelerating the demise of the Turks in the Middle East. When the promised independence was, instead, replaced by a mandate of a Western power, they were sorely dismayed and open rebellion ensued in the following years. In spite of these setbacks the Syrians, nevertheless, pledged their support for France when World War II broke out in 1939. Syrian independence was finally recognized in 1943.

Following WW II Syria was plagued by serious and long lasting political instability. There were frequent clashes with Israel and numerous military coups d'etats from 1945 until 1958 when a broad, but ill-fated, union with Egypt was forged. The so-called United Arab Republic (UAR), with the charismatic Jamal Adel Nasser as its president, survived less than four years.

Disenchantment with and alienation from the West moved Syria into the orbit of influence of the USSR, who was eager to secure a foothold in the strategic Middle East and to neutralize Syria's historic relationship with the West.

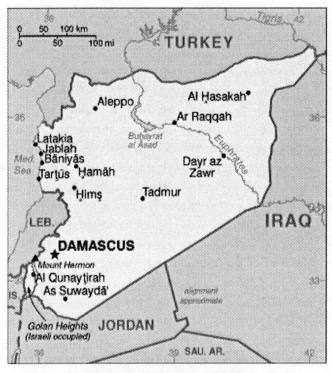

Syria & Lebanon - 2005
Courtesy of the University of Texas Libraries

Unrest and turmoil continued in Syria until power was seized in November 1970 by Hafez Al Assad, who established an iron clad regime, effectively suppressing all forms of dissent. His firm and ruthless crushing of the uprising by the Muslim Brotherhood in the city of Hama in 1982 reinforced his credentials as an authoritarian ruler who would not tolerate any form of opposition. Syria participated in three major wars with Israel, losing to Israel in 1967 the strategic Golan Heights, a hilly area of 485 square miles in the southwest corner of Syria.

In 1976 Syria intervened in the Lebanese civil war that raged, off and on, until 1990. Instrumental in neutralizing the opposing militant factions and imposing a degree of stability, their presence in Lebanon continued way past any real need, nearly 30 years, during which time they wielded substantial influence over both political and economic matters. Following the assassination of former Lebanese Prime Minister Rafiq Hariri in February 2005, an act widely implicating Syria, and faced with widespread international pressure, Syria withdrew its presence from Lebanon. Although, by May 2005 it had removed its 15,000 troops and extensive intelligence networks, it remains to be seen to what extent it has retained a high degree of influence in Lebanese affairs through the possibly wide spectrum of Lebanese contacts and associates who no doubt have benefited from Syrian patronage over the years.

Although the ruling party in Syria is Baath, as it was in Iraq under Saddam Hussein, it is a different brand of socialism and historically the two countries have found themselves on the opposite ends of a polarized Middle East. So much so that President Assad even joined the Western coalition against Iraq during the first Gulf War in 1990-91.

Acting as something of a spoiler in the Arab-Israeli peace discussions, Syria has consistently frustrated any peace arrangement that does not promise, up front, the return of the entire Golan Heights.

Syria has been labeled as one of a handful of countries that 'supports terrorism.' This ominous distinction stems from its accommodation to groups advocating violent resistance to Israeli occupation, and for its support of and possible control over Hezbollah, a predominantly Shiite organization based in Lebanon, supported by Iran, and dedicated to the removal of Israeli and any other foreign presence from Lebanon—and by any means possible.

Today there are close to 425,000 Palestinians in Syria—mainly in and around Damascus—of which as many as 110,000 are still in refugee camps. Syria is also widely accused by the Western Coalition of facilitating the movement of Muslim insurgents across the Syrian-Iraqi border to wage an insurgency against the western military presence in Iraq, an accusation that the Syrian leadership continues to deny.

The government of Bashar Al Assad is clearly under intense pressure today, both internally and internationally. To a large extent its ability to survive the current crisis will depend on the final outcome the UN's investigation of its alleged involvement in the assassination of Lebanon's former Prime Minister and on what surfaces regarding its role in the movement of fighters into Iraq. It is doubtful that the current regime could long endure international isolation and concerted UN sanctions.

Little Lebanon

Lebanon has been the darling of the Middle East even before it became an independent country. For decades its beautiful topography, agreeable climate and open society has been a magnet for business leaders, government officials and eager vacationers. Throughout its history it has been one of the more progressive areas of the region, but alas, not insulated from the many turbulent, often violent, winds that seem to rage in the Middle East.

Smaller than the state of Connecticut, which is itself the third smallest state in the U.S., and boasting today no more than four million people, it has been a key regional transportation and trading center for several thousand years. Like every country in the area, the land which is now Lebanon has seen many conquerors, occupiers and sojourners in its long history. Greeks, Romans, Arabs, Ottoman and Seljuk Turks, European Crusaders and Western colonial powers all played a role in shaping what Lebanon is today, from a sociological, ethnic, religious and economic perspective.

Perhaps a good place to start Lebanon's history is about 2500 BC with the Phoenicians, a Semitic people probably descendant of the Canaanites, who lived along the coastline on the eastern end of the Mediterranean Sea. Occupied and reoccupied countless times by regional powers they somehow managed to flourish, eventually achieving a degree of self rule and evolving into a notable seafaring nation and founding numerous colonies around the Mediterranean. Aside from its success as a maritime and trading giant, many advances are accorded the Phoenicians, including the alphabet, invention of glass and the manufacture of textiles, metal and glass.

The Romans ruled Lebanon for nearly 600 years, leaving behind significant signs of their past glory, much of which is still in evidence today. Lebanon suffered the same fate of foreign domination and occupation as most other states in the area with one exception. In Lebanon there seems to have been a good deal more assimilation with the invaders. Today the ethnic composition of much of the indigenous population is a testament to the settlement and intermarriage that apparently took place in past centuries, the diversity no doubt yielding great dividends.

Under the Ottoman Turks who ruled for about 400 years a good deal of autonomy was granted and delegated to prominent local families. The consecutive dynasties of Maan and Shihab together lasted from 1516 to 1697. Both families were from the Druze Sect, a protestant offshoot of Islam, with the latter family eventually converting to Maronite Catholicism.

Lebanon's 19th and 20th century history has been scarred by sectarian strife, often bloody massacres and civil war. In the 1800s it was primarily between the Druze and the Christians; in the 1900s the conflict widened to include virtually all so-called confessional (i.e. religious) groups.

After World War I the French were awarded the Mandate for Lebanon and administered the country until its independence in 1943. It was the intention of the colonial powers to establish a country, ostensibly to protect the Christian community, but also to secure a friendly state with 'like mind' in the strategic Middle East.

Post independence there were perhaps two noteworthy events which worked to create great strife, turmoil and destruction. Lebanon's system of government is somewhat unique in that it attempts to share power on a formula which recognizes the proportional make-up of the population. In accordance with its 1926 constitution and based on a census around the 1930s, Christian Maronites, which constituted the largest sect, are entitled to the highest and most powerful governmental office, the presidency. Likewise, the post of Prime Minister is filled by a Sunni Muslim and the president of parliament by a Shiite Muslim. And so it is throughout government, with positions meted out, more or less, on a proportional basis. The system seemed to work reasonably well until there occurred major shifts in the make-up of the population and hence an imbalance in representation. Although there has been no recent census, it is apparent that the Muslim growth rate has far exceeded that of the Christians, a disparity that has hardly been corrected in the political system.

The second event was the flight of hundreds of thousands of Palestinian refugees to Lebanon after the 1948 and 1967 wars with Israel. In 1948 alone some 150,000 Palestinians took refuge in Lebanon at the time when Lebanon's entire population was not much more that 1.5 million. Most of these fleeing Palestinians were Muslim, exacerbating the delicate internal confessional balance. Today there are some 400,000 Palestinians in Lebanon with close to half still in camps. This demographic shift contributed in a significant way to the chaos and tension that led to the bloody civil war that started in 1975 and raged off and on for 15 years, bringing the country to its knees economically, politically and socially. During those turbulent years, by invitation of the Lebanese government in 1976, the Syrians intervened in Lebanon to help stop the fighting. They remained long after hostilities ceased, exerting overriding political and economic power over Lebanon until international pressure forced their withdrawal in 2005 after the assassination of former Prime Minister Rafik Harriri. The Israeli invasion in 1982, in retaliation for Palestinian raids into Israel from southern Lebanon, created additional destruction and significant loss of life, by some counts in excess of 15,000, mainly civilians. The Palestinian threat in Lebanon also gave Israel the excuse to establish a so-called buffer zone on Lebanese soil, purportedly to foil future attacks on northern Israel. This buffer constituted some 16% of the land area of Lebanon and was the stimulant that led to the creation of Hezbollah, a militant group dedicated to the removal of all foreign presence from Lebanon. Their continual attacks on the Israelis and their allies in the buffer zone, if not directly causing, certainly contributed in a significant way to the Israeli withdrawal in the year 2000.

Lebanon boasts extensive and progressive educational systems, financial institutions, recreation, sports and the arts. Its open door policies have attracted many visitors and immigrants of all persuasions. In the past this has not always worked in Lebanon's best interest as subversive groups were also able to establish themselves with relative ease, making Lebanon itself a target of states or groups that espoused differing views. Israel frequently punished Lebanon and its people for harboring Palestinian resistance groups by, for example, destroying electric power generation stations and other infrastructure and on one occasion destroying Middle East Airlines' entire commercial fleet of 13 jet aircraft on the ground at Beirut International Airport.

Although there continues to be sectarian tensions and varying groups struggling for more power, the year 2005 saw a growing sense of patriotism, coalesced by the assassination of Rafik Harriri, an act allegedly committed with Syrian implication. Hezbollah has a key role to play in Lebanon's future. While labeled as a terrorist group by the US, it has evolved into a well organized political and social entity, and an active and democratic participant in government affairs. The concern is that it also remains a well armed paramilitary organization; a situation that was allowed to persist as long as there was Israeli occupation of Lebanese lands. Although Israel withdrew from the so-called 'Buffer Zone' in south Lebanon in 2000, the tiny Sheba Farms, which Lebanon considers its land, iş still occupied by Israel, giving Hezbollah the excuse it needs to continue in this earlier defensive role. Enjoying substantial support from both Syria and Iran, there is fear that Hezbollah loyalties are split. Will they play a constructive role promoting unity and stability in Lebanon or will they do the bidding of other powers? 2006 could be a watershed year.

Lebanon has made a valiant attempt to return to its earlier days of glory as a financial capital, a vacation Mecca, an educational center and an open society for free thought and self-expression. Regrettably, success or failure often is more dependent on the level of interference or restraint by its neighbors and overall regional stability than on the expressed desires and concerted efforts of the Lebanese.

Juggling Jordan

Jordan, a small desert kingdom nestled in between a vast Saudi Arabia, a volatile Iraq, an unfriendly Syria and an intimidating Israel, owes its existence to the foresight or folly of the British and the French. After World War I ended and based on recommendations in the Sykes-Picot Agreement, these two victorious powers took it upon themselves to carve out new and rather arbitrary political entities in the region that was formerly a part of the Ottoman Empire. While the territory west of the Jordan River became Palestine, that east of the Jordan River was called Transjordan and mandated by the League of Nations to Britain to administer. The name, Transjordan, was shortened to 'Jordan' in 1950.

In 1921, as a reward for helping defeat the Turks, Abdullah, a son of the Hashemite Sherif Hussein of Mecca, was made the Emir of Transjordan. King Hussein, who ruled Jordan from 1952 until his death in 1999 was the grandson of Abdullah. Abdullah II, the present king, is Hussein's eldest son. Transjordan did not obtain full independence from Britain until 1946.

The early history of Jordan mirrors that of the contiguous regions. Numerous invaders of many stripes came and went, leaving their traces in the desert sands, remnants of large cities, now skeletons against the stark beauty of the shifting dunes.

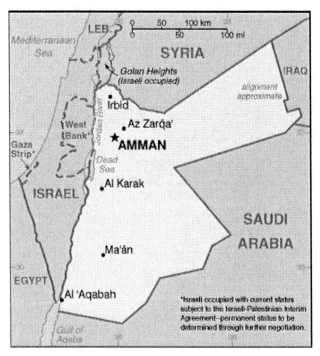

The Kingdom of Jordan - 2005
Courtesy of the University of Texas Libraries

After the war with newly founded Israel in 1948, in which a large part of Arab Palestine was lost to Israel, Jordan annexed the West Bank and offered its residents Jordanian citizenship. Tensions with Israel, always unsettled, reached a new high in 1967, prompting Israel to initiate a brief but devastating war against Syria, Egypt and Jordan. Their rapid victory left Israel in control of the entire West Bank, including East Jerusalem, which it continues to occupy as of this writing. This war generated more refugees some of whom fled to Jordan, putting great hardship on the economy of a small country with limited economic capability. It is reckoned that Jordan today accommodates over 1.7 million Palestinians with over 280,000 still living in refugee camps—this for a country with a total population of just over 5.5 million.

Out of the Palestinian presence in Jordan grew several resistance movements, for the most part, under the leadership of Yasser Arafat. Their frequent raids against the Israelis in the Occupied Territories stimulated retaliatory attacks on Jordan and often conflicted with Jordan's own political policies. By 1970 the armed Palestinian presence was seen as a growing threat to King Hussein's rule and to Jordanian sovereignty, prompting Jordanian troops in September of that year to wage an all out war against the Palestinian militant groups and forcing them eventually to relocate from Jordan to Lebanon.

Jordan participated in a modest way in the 1973 war initiated by Egypt against Israel and in 1974 acknowledged the Palestinian Liberation Organization (PLO) as the sole representative of the Palestinian people. In 1988 it renounced its claim to the West Bank and supported the creation of a Palestinian state along side Israel. In 1994 Jordan became the second Arab nation (after Egypt) to sign a Peace Treaty with Israel, thus, for the first time, normalizing relations between the two neighbors who share their largest border with one another.

Although Jordan cannot compete with other Middle East countries economically, it has, particularly through the enlightened leadership of King Hussein, exerted a significant and moderating influence on regional politics. During his reign of some 47 turbulent years, the Monarch managed to survive many challenges to his leadership (and his life) while, most of the time, maintaining cordial relations with most of his neighbors, and particularly with the West.

Jordan has been severely rocked by the turmoil and

instability in the Middle East. With few natural resources and a limited industrial base, to survive economically, it has had to depend largely on financial aid and accommodation from its Arab neighbors and, to a lesser extent, from the West. Therefore, no doubt its political posture must be fashioned with the potential economic ramifications clearly in mind. It's hard to see that dilemma changing very much in the foreseeable future.

Secluded Saudi Arabia

Allah hu Akbar is the cry from the top of the minaret, calling the righteous to prayer five times a day; a beautiful chant ringing through the cool desert night air, reaching equally the ears of the young and old, the Saudi and foreigner. God is great. This seems to be the hallmark, the call sign of a country entrusted with the two most holy shrines in all of Islam, and yet it is a chant that often wreaks fear, its use and misuse by martyrs waging 'jihad' in the name of God.

No one paid much attention to Saudi Arabia prior to the discovery of oil in the early 1930s. Except for the annual pilgrimage to Mecca it was not so much a destination as it was a route bridging the Mediterranean and the Orient. A people called the Sabeans inhabited southwestern Arabia and became prosperous in the trade of incenses and spices. The Nabataeans controlled the trade routes through Jordan and along the western coast of Arabia. It was a poor and forbidding tribal land eventually coupled together by the courage and fortitude of one man, Abdel Aziz Ibn Saud, whose sons have continued to rule the country since his death in 1953.

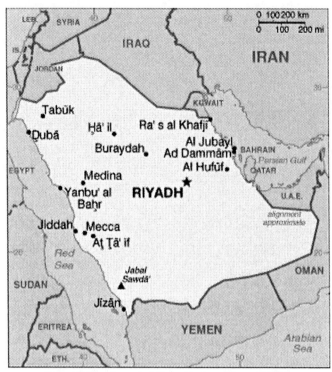

The Kingdom of Saudi Arabia - 2005
Courtesy of the University of Texas Libraries

In the mid-1700's an ancestor of Abdel Aziz, Muhammad Ibn Saud, forged an alliance with a radical fundamentalist by the name of Mohammad Ibn Abdel Wahab with the objective of unifying the diverse nomadic tribes that roamed the desert. Abdel Wahab was a fiery reformer who advocated strict observance of Islamic tradition and rigid 'Hanbali' law. His influence was widespread in Arabia, and highly pervasive. This alliance was instrumental in establishing the overall character and being of the kingdom, an influence that is very much in evidence in Arabia even today. Those in Arabia at present who take strong and very vocal exception to western customs and foreign presence on their soil can trace this zeal back to Abdel Wahab. In recent times this pact between the ruling Saudi royal family and the religious followers of this extreme form of Islam, referred to as "Wahabis", has been sorely tested, particularly since the first Gulf war of 1990-91 when a coalition of mainly western troops landed on Saudi soil to repel the advances of Saddam Hussein into Kuwait. The ruling family has often compromised on policies to appease, or at least avoid alienating, the religious factions. The balance has become more precarious as pressures mount from the terrorist attacks in the United States on 9/11/2001, which have spilled over to random acts of terror within the borders of the Kingdom.

When one speaks of Saudi Arabia, one thinks of oil. 25% of the world's known oil resources are under the sands of Saudi Arabia. It is the largest crude oil exporter and, with the largest spare crude oil production capacity, it has been able to act as a stabilizing influence on world oil markets—when it's in its interest to do so. The connection between Saudi Arabia and the United States, dating back to World War II, has been productive and mutually beneficial. The US has provided the lion's share of the technical know-how needed to find, develop and produce Saudi crude and has been an important market for the product. In return, Saudi Arabia has tended to adopt a conciliatory posture within OPEC and has been successful in moderating oil price demands and production targets of the cartel. The US has also been the chief weapons supplier to the Kingdom and the recipient of large deposits of Saudi capital. In the aftermath of 9/11 that relationship has been sorely tested. With 15 of the 19 highjackers Saudi nationals, that long friendship has been hotly questioned. Is the Royal family really in control of the country? Does it represent the will of the people? Do they profess friendship on the one hand while, on the other, supporting terror acts against the US?

The recent formal ascension to the throne by Crown Prince Abdullah, after having in effect ruled the country since his brother, King Fahd, suffered a stroke ten years ago, should insure that the close relationship will be maintained, at least for the foreseeable future. Clearly, there is an essential mutual benefit from close collaboration and cooperation. America needs the oil and a strategic friend in the heart of the Arab world; Saudi Arabia needs the oil outlet, American arms and U. S. support against the forces that would unseat the ruling family.

Meanwhile, the Kingdom has moved quietly to introduce a number of meaningful economic and some baby-step political reforms. The climate for foreign investment has markedly improved in the last few years, and particularly with Saudi admission into the World Trade Organization (WTO) in December 2005. Thanks to the oil price surges of 2004-2006 progress in infrastructure development and in oil related industries such as petrochemicals is booming. The so-called 'Shoura' or consultative assembly, while first muted in the 1970s has finally been more formally introduced and is functioning, demanding more say-so in certain state matters such as budgetary issues. In late 2005, for the first time, women stood for election in the Chamber of Commerce and some were elected. While still denied many opportunities available in most other Islamic countries, progress on women issues is evident and education for women is both widespread and intensive. No doubt the improved economic environment reduces somewhat the social strains on a country boasting a rapidly growing population, half of which is under the age of 20 and scrounging for employment.

The big challenge facing the Saudi Ruling family, authoritative but with a growing bent towards reform, is how to continue to manage the precarious balance between the westernized business and academic community and the conservative Islamists who have traditionally occupied an important position, and still wield considerable influence over government policies, especially in the fields of religion, education and law. However, terror acts committed by Islamic radicals in the Kingdom in the last few years has enabled the ruling family to take bolder measures against the substantial Wahabi influence. Nevertheless, care is taken to maintain a conciliatory working relationship.

Pivotal Palestine

The land in and around Palestine has received far in excess of its share of world history. A country about the size of New Hampshire, it is a land with probably too much history and too little geography. It has been a country blest with the three great religions and yet cursed by them; a land that has been a battlefield and burial ground countless times. It is a part of the world seemingly in perpetual turmoil, turmoil that continues to this day unabated.

What is it about Palestine that has attracted such discord? What is the history of this place? Starting back in biblical times, the Jews ruled all or part of the land now called Palestine during several periods prior to the coming of Jesus Christ.

Between the 11th and 7th centuries BC during the lives of Joshua, and Kings Saul, David and Solomon.

Between 145-63 BC in Judah, the southern sector of Palestine.

Before, in between and after it was ruled at one time or the other by Amorites, Canaanites, Assyrians, Babylonians, Persians, Greeks, Romans, Muslim Arabs, Christian Crusaders, and Egyptian Mamelukes, Ottoman Turks, and the British under a UN mandate. Since 1967 it has been occupied totally by the Jewish state of Israel.

Aside from the Jewish kings, armies of the world's greatest leaders and conquerors have invaded this land, from King Cyrus of Persia, to Alexander the Great, Julius Caesar, and Emperor Napoleon. The Palestinians now living in Israel or in the Occupied Territories trace their origins there back hundreds if not thousands of years. Their fortunes rose and fell with the successes and failures of those empires that ruled over them. Most Palestinian's converted to Islam, although they were not compelled to do so by the early Islamic conquerors. Today there is a sizable minority of Palestinians who are Christian.

The territory of Palestine was under the rule of the Ottoman Empire for some 400 years, ending after World War I. It was recognized as a political entity after the breakup of this Empire when Great Britain was asked by the League of Nations to administer it as a mandate until it was able to administer itself. The Ottoman Turks had divided Palestine into several 'sanjaks' or districts, the administration of which was placed primarily in the hands of the Arab population during which time every 'revealed' religion, Jewish, Christian and Muslim, was allowed a large measure of freedom of worship and autonomy

During WW I the Arabs had been promised independence for Palestine as a reward for their active involvement and support in ousting the Ottoman Turks. The creation of the British mandate was a major disappointment and a significant setback for the Arab independence movement. Later, in its so-called "White Paper" of 1939, Britain made a commitment to establish an independent Palestinian state within ten years. This was to be a state inclusive of Muslims, Jews and Christians. Of course this dream was never realized. Today the conflict in the Holy Land is not a religious struggle between Muslim and Jew; it is a political struggle for an immigrant Jewish state versus an indigenous Palestinian Arab state.

ISRAEL in Biblical Times

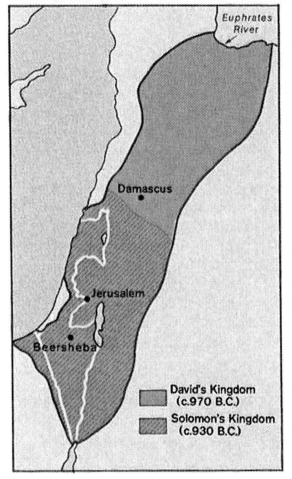

Israel in Biblical Times
Map courtesy of University of Texas Libraries

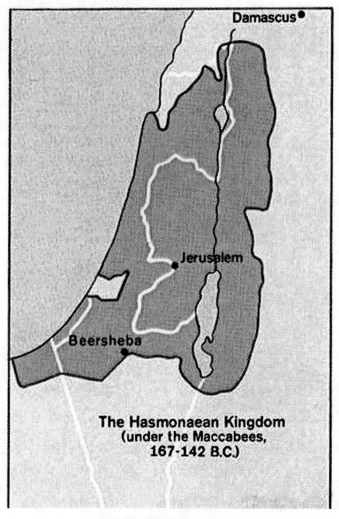

Israel in Biblical Times
Map courtesy of University of Texas Libraries

The United Nations partition of Palestine in 1947, the declaration of Israeli independence and the ensuing wars with their Arab neighbors were covered in earlier chapters. Suffice it to say here that neither side has known real peace or security in nearly 100 years of contiguity.

No discussion of modern day Palestine can be complete without mention of Yasser Arafat who was the controversial but undisputed representative of the Palestinian people for nearly forty years. A freedom fighter, a guerilla, a statesman, a leader, a terrorist, a Nobel Peace prize recipient, a survivor, a father figure for a displaced people—who exactly was this man?

Arafat claimed to have been born in Jerusalem, fled Gaza during the 1948-9 war and ended up in Egypt where he dabbled in politics while earning a degree in engineering. In the early 1960s he helped found the Fatah movement, a nationalistic entity dedicated to military opposition of Israel. He organized raids into Israel and solicited international support for Palestinian resistance to the Israeli state. In 1968 he joined the Palestinian Liberation Organization, the PLO, an umbrella organization encompassing and unifying 11 different resistance groups, including Fatah which became its dominant member. With the Palestinians in exile his power base, Arafat soon became the leader of the PLO. In the early 1970s he was forced by King Hussein to flee his bases in Jordan where he had operated with impunity, often embarrassing the King who objected to many of the PLO actions. Upon leaving Jordan, Arafat reorganized in Lebanon and, within a few years, had established a large, well-armed insurgent group there, from which raids into Israel continued. The PLO presence in Lebanon soon upset the delicate confessional balance that had existed for decades and contributed in a significant way to the

Lebanese civil war that erupted in 1975.

By 1974 Arafat had gained broad Arab backing and much international support, leading to his invitation to address the United Nations in New York. In his speech to the General Assembly he declared that he held an olive branch in one hand and a freedom fighter's rifle in the other, and admonished the international community not to let the olive branch fall from his hand. History must judge at who's doorstep must lay the blame that the rifle won out over the olive branch. The PLO and its splinter groups were directly or indirectly behind a long list of highjackings, assassinations, and bombings, becoming a major irritant not only to Israel but also the international community. These actions propelled the Palestinian struggle into the global limelight, but did not earn the Palestinians a great deal of sympathy or support.

The Israeli invasion of Lebanon in 1982 again forced Arafat to relocate, this time to Tunisia where it was assumed he would be forgotten or at least marginalized. A man of uncanny political skills and popularity, far from disappearing from the scene, Arafat's strength and influence only increased, each defeat somehow translating into glory for him and adoration from his people.

1988 was a historic year in Palestinian-Israeli relations. At long last the PLO finally recognized Israel's right to exist, held democratic elections and began to organize itself in what, at first, looked like an orderly fashion. Alas, whatever talents Arafat had in politics he seems to have lacked in administration. Although Arafat himself apparently lived a simple, even austere life, corruption and cronyism allegedly abounded in his government and even today vast sums of government money are unaccounted for.

The Middle East Peace Accords, brokered by President

Clinton, was a period of hope when both the Israelis under the leadership of Prime Minister Yitzhak Rabin and the Palestinians under the direction of Chairman Yasser Arafat displayed a genuine commitment to work together for peace in the region. The rapport the two leaders had with each other provided the chemistry needed to resolve differences across the table rather than on the hills of battle. The unfortunate assassination of Rabin in 1995 by an Israeli extremist ended that spirit of cooperation. The world rather universally condemns Arafat for not seizing the settlement offer later made by Prime Minister Barak in 2000, a proposal better than had ever been tabled before, or since. As is discussed later, as attractive as the offer seemed, several very crucial matters were left unaddressed, matters that no Arab leader could easily omit without dire consequences at home. Perhaps the greater failure was in not continuing the dialogue.

The international community seems to place the blame for the 'Second Intifada', or the second popular uprising against the occupation, on Arafat's shoulders. By 2000 delays in implementation and violations of the provisions of the Peace Accords had heightened tensions between the Israelis and the Palestinians to dangerous levels. The spark that finally ignited the Intifada was prompted by then Minister Ariel Sharon's unwelcome trek to the Holy Islamic sites with a sizable contingent of bodyguards. Subsequent Israeli incursions into the West Bank routed Arafat's security forces, destroyed his communications network and transportation means and imprisoned him in his compound for nearly three years, until his death in 2004. During this period he was accused of not reining in and controlling the various militant groups attacking Israel. While there is much to criticize in Arafat's actions, it's hard to conclude exactly how Israeli actions enhanced his ability to control anything or encourage cooperation. Clearly, he had become disillusioned with prospects for peace, particularly with the aggressive policies of the governing Likud party and his long time nemesis, Prime Minister Sharon. Even if a will existed, growing impatience and frustration among the more militant Palestinian factions were a mounting reality unto themselves. These groups were beginning to exhibit scant loyalty to a leader who seemed powerless to halt Israeli settlement expansion, military occupation and subjugation.

In death Arafat's popularity has not abated. But how will history judge him? For sure Arafat cast a long shadow on events in the Middle East for many years. His dream of a sovereign Palestinian State was never achieved in his lifetime. Did he really advance that cause or retard it? What will be his legacy? Will he be remembered as a visionary or a villain, a reluctant terrorist or an inept peacemaker?

Arafat's successor in power, Mahmoud Abbas, has inherited a number of whopping challenges. Pursuing a peace plan with Israel that will meet the test of acceptability to the Palestinians, providing security and control where little has existed for decades, setting up an efficient administration, transparent and free of corruption, reining in and establishing control over the various militant organizations with diverse views and varying agendas, rebuilding the country's infrastructure, educational and social systems—just to name a few. Perhaps his first and maybe most important challenge is to shake off the legacy of cronyism and corruption and to bring in fresh new, educated and enlightened Palestinians who will work towards the building of a peaceful, progressive and unified government.

Following the unilateral decision of the Sharon government to withdraw from the Gaza Strip, the administration of

President George W. Bush now seems committed to seize this opportunity and use it as the first step in forging a lasting settlement. Success will depend on the resolution of many thorny issues including the ability of the Palestinians to evolve a responsible government that will work for the good of the people and the willingness of the Israelis to compromise on some key issues regarding the Arab refugees, the Jewish settlements and the granting of real sovereignty to the emerging political entity.

The ascension to power of Hamas in the elections held in January 2006 has further complicated, and perhaps setback significantly, the likelihood of near term progress on a peace settlement. To date Hamas has refused to recognize Israel, to renounce violence or to accept those agreements reached to date with the Israelis. Absent the acceptance of these non-negotiable conditions has isolated the Hamas government internationally and is creating serious internal strains within the Palestinian community.

The Palestinian Dilemma

In a nutshell the current dilemma in Palestine is its unsuccessful struggle to regain lost lands. It's that and all the other implications and complications of a military occupation. In spite of how simple the problem and how straightforward the solution, the issue remains unresolved after nearly 39 years. In fact each year an acceptable resolution seems to recede further into an even darker future. If we can assume that the Palestinian objective is to establish a peaceful, free and sovereign state comprising the West Bank, Gaza and a piece of East Jerusalem, then their cause takes on a rather simple and straightforward character, and it would seem to be entirely warranted. However, pursuit of a just resolution has been flawed. Political and diplomatic efforts have failed, wars were unsuccessful, Arab pressure ineffectual and violent resistance, call it terrorism, has been counter productive. Meanwhile, as settlements in the occupied territories continue to expand, as the occupied people become more and more desperate and as blood continues to be shed on both sides, thoughts and deeds become more and more entrenched, further complicating what started out as a rather simple early fix.

The Zionist movement encourages the ingathering of all Jews into Israel. To accommodate such an influx, more room, more land becomes pretty vital. The Likud party strategy seems to mirror this dream. The Israeli past policy of establishing and expanding Jewish settlements on the occupied territories does not bode well for a just resolution involving the return of Palestinian land in exchange for peace. The building of and support for the 200 odd settlements in the occupied territories, the investment that these entail and the drain on Israel's economy in sustaining and protecting them do not leave one with an impression that there is serious intention to ever surrender these territories back to the Arabs. On the contrary, it would seem that the net effect of the settlement policy has been to frustrate the peace process. Until the unilateral Israeli withdrawal from Gaza in 2005 this situation was worsening. In the last ten years the number of Jewish settlers in the West Bank and Gaza had increased 95%, to well over 200,000. Settlements have been a particularly thorny issue. Thomas Friedman, the well informed and very objective journalist who regularly contributes Op-Ed pieces in the New York Times, in several of his writings, has singled out the settlements issue as a most disturbing and provocative act and a hindrance to peace. Having said this, Mr. Sharon's decision to withdraw all 21 settlements from Gaza and 4 from the West Bank was a welcomed, though perhaps an unexpected, development. It presented both a challenge as well as an opportunity for an evolution towards a genuine and lasting peaceful coexistence between two peoples that have suffered much too long together.

The recent so-called "Security Fence" now under construction creates another serious barrier to peace. By some estimates, when the fence is completed, around 10% of the West Bank will fall on the Israeli side of the fence, including some of the most fertile agricultural land and water resources.

As of 2005 over 80,000 olive and citrus trees had already been uprooted and 37 kilometers of water pipes ripped up and some 30,000 farmers cut off from their orchards and farms. Thousands are separated from their families, their schools and their work and movement between areas is extremely tedious, complex and uncertain.

Typically, Palestinian reaction has been to lash out in some fashion, to fight back in any way they can. But radical Arab or Islamic groups, who have committed acts of terror around the world in the name of Palestinian grief, have not furthered the Palestinian cause. On the contrary these acts only divert attention from the core issue. The focus inevitably shifts from restoration of Arab lands and the lifting of occupation to an issue of Israel's security.

Some observers have concluded that the Palestinian aim to remove total Israeli presence from the occupied territories is pretty much unattainable. They express their frustration like this: When there is no form of resistance, Israel has no real reason to withdraw; When Palestinians do mount resistance, Israel has reason to stay.

Ariel Sharon's decision to unilaterally withdraw entirely from Gaza and to close down several West Bank settlements was a welcomed move, assuming it would be a full and genuine withdrawal and not constitute a pretext to do no more than that. For whatever the motivation, this move has certainly provided an opportunity to observe whether the Palestinians are able to organize and administer a stable and responsible government, a regime that will be a reliable partner for peace. The successor to Arafat as president of the Palestinian Authority, Mr. Mahmoud Abbas, tried to piece together a credible security force that would ensure compliance with the cease fire that had been agreed with Israel, rid the administration of widespread corruption and to work out an accommodation with the more militant groups of Hamas and Islamic Jihad, while at the same time unifying the Palestinian people under his leadership. This was a truly an ambitious goal for a man who has spent his entire career in the giant shadow of Arafat. Any one of these would have been daunting all by itself. His success depended on the eagerness of the Palestinians to make a paradigm shift in their lives, international recognition, support and encouragement that is essential, and the extent that the Israeli leadership was willing to work closely and responsively with him. Regrettably, few of these challenges have yielded any notable result. Not only has Hamas gained broad support within the Palestinian territories as a legitimate alternative political entity but it scored a major victory in the January 2006 parliamentary elections, earning for itself the right to appoint the new government. Meanwhile, the Fatah movement itself is in disarray with the "Young Turks" within the party challenging the "Old Guard" for greater voice and participation. As of this writing the viability of the Hamas government is in question with Israel and the United States threatening to refuse recognition unless Hamas acknowledges Israel's right to exist, renounces the use of violence and accepts the peace steps thus far concluded with Israel. Moreover, Israel is refusing to fork over Palestinian funds which are collected by Israel and the U.S. is threatening to withhold all aid. Without funds the government, indeed the country, will no doubt descend into chaos. For its part Hamas has the opportunity to prove itself the able administrator and benefactor of the people it claims to be. This will require some serious compromises on ingrained policies and the restoration of law and order. Meanwhile the Israeli elections in late March 2006 formally brought to power the caretaker Olmert government, whose brand new 'Kadima' party had already campaigned on its intention to impose unilateral borders with the West Bank. Indeed, there are many that believe it was Prime Minister Sharon's objective to do just that, with the permanent boundary defined by the separation barrier currently being built around Israel. But peace in the region will require more than the delineation of a border. The refugee issue must be resolved and the spin-off Palestinian state must be made viable both economically and politically. Tall orders that will require more statesmanship and, yes, more courage, sacrifice and risk-taking than we have yet witnessed.

The Peace Process

For too long peace in the Middle East has been more a pious prayer than a probable prospect.

The so-called peace process can be characterized as one step forward and two steps backwards. Following the Six Day War in 1967 the UN passed resolution 242 calling for the withdrawal of the Israeli military presence from the territories occupied in that war. In its preamble, it states, "*Emphasizing the inadmissibility of acquisition of territory by war* and the need to work for a just and lasting peace in which every state in the area can live in security."

Following the 1973 war waged by Egypt to recover the Sinai, UN resolution 338 was passed, again reiterating the imperative that Israel withdraws from those territories occupied in 1967. It is with these resolutions that the Arabs, and presumably the UN, expect Israel to comply. Some suggest that the Palestinian territories now controlled by Israel are not 'occupied' territories; they are 'disputed' territories, since there was no Palestinian political entity in 1967 when Israel occupied them. It is true that the West Bank had been incorporated into Jordan after the 1948 war. However, if a dispute does exist today concerning these territories, it would seem to be between Jordan and those that aspire for a Palestinian state and perhaps a resolution should best be left to those parties alone. In fact, Jordan relinquished its claim on the West Bank in 1988 and supported the establishment of an independent Palestinian state. In any event, whether one labels those areas 'disputed' or 'occupied' would seem irrelevant to the spirit of the resolutions calling for a return to pre-1967 borders.

Anwar Sadat, the then president of Egypt, made a historical, unprompted visit to Jerusalem in 1977 in a quest for peace. This initiative shocked other Arab countries who saw it as a betrayal of the unified Arab stand and a weakening of their bargaining position. Egypt was clearly the largest and most feared foe of Israel and with its neutralization the other Arab states were even more powerless. For several years Egypt's relations with its Arab neighbors were sorely strained. The Sadat overture eventually resulted in the so-called Camp David Peace Accord between Egypt and Israel in September 1978, leading to the signing of a formal agreement on March 26, 1979. The peace agreement with Jordan was not concluded until 1994, after progress had been made in the Oslo Peace Accords. As of this writing no other Arab country has entered into a formal peace arrangement with Israel.

Another important milestone on the road to peace occurred in 1988. The Palestinian Liberation Organization, the 'PLO,' held democratic elections for its representative assembly and passed resolutions that, for the very first time, accepted UN resolution 181, 242 and 338. This was a truly ground breaking event since the Palestinians now, at long last, formally accepted the UN partition of Palestine and the presence of Israel as an independent state. The PLO, with Yasser Arafat as president, was recognized as the legitimate representative of the Palestinian people by 104 countries. The elections were observed by an international monitoring group that included former president Jimmy Carter, who attested to the fairness and legitimacy of those elections. It is somewhat ironic that Yasser Arafat was virtually the only leader in the Arab world to have been elected in a fair and democratic fashion, and, yet, it was only he who, in his last days, that the Americans and Israelis refused to recognize and tried to marginalize, an effort which only seemed to increase his popularity among the Palestinians.

The period of 1991-1998 can be remembered as a budding period of hope. It started with the so-called Madrid Peace conference (from which the PLO was excluded), then the Oslo Accords, the Interim Agreement and the Wye River Agreements. At least the two sides were talking to each other. In general terms, these agreements called for a step-by-step withdrawal of the Israeli presence from certain parts of the occupied territories, and the granting of autonomy to the Palestinians for handling certain administrative responsibilities. Defense, foreign policy, resource allocation, etc. were to remain in Israeli control and there was no promise of statehood. Moreover, highly sensitive issues like the status of Jerusalem, the Palestinian refugees and the Israeli settlements in the occupied territories were left for later resolution. Nevertheless, the agreements were viewed as progress, steps in the right direction. Unfortunately, discussions took too long and implementation was too slow. On both sides there were violations, delays in implementation and excuses for non-compliance. These led to disappointments and restlessness on both sides.

In year 2000, with the encouragement of President Clinton, Israeli Prime Minister Barak offered the Palestinians more than they had ever been offered before. Although the proposal was never debated or approved by the Knesset, the Israeli parliament, it was the first time the Palestinians had ever been promised withdrawal from most of the West Bank and Gaza, statehood and a piece of East Jerusalem. However sweet it seemed, in the Arab mind the deal was still deficient in some significant areas. The refugee problem, over a million displaced Palestinians and a most sensitive issue, was not adequately addressed, many Israeli settlements would remain on Palestinian land and the new Arab state would have no control over some pretty important sovereign rights like its own defense, its airspace, its water resources and control over its own borders. As offered, the new state of Palestine could not have attained political or economic viability. Nevertheless, the offer represented an excellent place to begin negotiations. That it was not pursued more exhaustively by the parties will remain in the minds of many historians as a genuinely missed opportunity. Someone once said that the Palestinians never miss an opportunity to miss an opportunity; a criticism no doubt widespread among all the players in the turbulent history of the Middle East.

The so-called "Second Intifada," which began in 2000, put an end to peace discussions. Perhaps it was the beginning of the end of hope. As discussed earlier, while Mr. Sharon's unwelcome march up to the Muslim Holy Sites was not the cause, it was certainly the spark that touched off the Second Intifada. (The word Intifada in Arabic translates as 'throwing of', meaning a struggle to terminate the occupation.) The First Intifada occurred in 1988, when mainly children and teenagers expressed their defiance of the Israeli military presence primarily by throwing stones at the Israeli troops stationed in the occupied territories. This proved to be a very visible method of resistance that received widespread publicity and a good deal of worldwide sympathy. The Second Intifada was uglier, for in the intervening period the Palestinians had managed to

obtain light arms and explosives that they used to press their determination to shed the yoke of occupation. The Temple Mount is the site of King Solomon's Temple, the second of which was destroyed by the Romans in about 90 AD. Since about 750 AD, called the Haram El Sharif, it has been the site of the Mosque of Omar or the "Dome of the Rock" and the Al-Aqsa Mosque, the third most holy place for Muslims, after Mecca and Medina. Ariel Sharon's unwelcomed visit with a large contingent of armed bodyguards was taken as an insult to Muslims everywhere. This action provoked open demonstrations by the Palestinians against the Israeli presence. These demonstrations were put down decisively by the Israeli troops. There was significant loss of life on both sides, particularly on the Palestinian side, and the matter quickly escalated into something of a mini war, albeit a war between military unequals. It is worth noting that the Intifada was an uprising of Palestinians, both Muslim and Christian, against occupation and had nothing to do with Islamic fundamentalism.

An observer might conclude that the rise in acts of terror and the proliferation of suicide bombers might have been born, or at least experienced a rebirth, in the aftermath of the fateful and untimely visit by Mr. Sharon.

Some hope for peace was revived with the unveiling of the so-called "Road Map" espoused by the US, Russia, the European Union and the United Nations, and specifically with President Bush's personal commitment to a final resolution. This was to be a guide leading to statehood for the Palestinians over a three year span, calling for the cessation of violence by the Palestinians, a pull back of Israeli troops from the West Bank and Gaza and returning the settlement population to where it was in March 2001. The more thorny issues of the core settlements, the right of return of refugees and the status of Jerusalem were all postponed for a later time. The parties continue to voice cautious support, while agonizing over the concessions that they each must accept. Of course, certain of the more radical groups on both sides continue to oppose and try to frustrate any peace agreement that does not, up front, recognize and accept those key elements considered by them to be non-negotiable. The challenge will be to marginalize these fringe groups and, however painful, to accept compromises. Regrettably, history does not provide a lot of encouragement in this area. However, in August 2005, the positive steps initially taken along this 'road' to peace were once again revived with the Bush administration, after a virtual absence of four years, making resolution of the Palestinian issue a priority. The sudden and untimely leadership change in Israel following Ariel Sharon's stroke could no doubt delay and further complicate progress towards real peace. On the other hand, Ehud Olmert who emerged as Prime Minister in the aftermath of the March 2006 elections has already telegraphed his intention to pursue a unilateral solution if peace initiatives are not reciprocated. We've been here before...

Prime Minister Sharon's plan for a unilateral withdrawal from the Gaza Strip which was announced in early 2004 and implemented in 2005 received mixed reviews from both the Arab and the Israeli sides. Many Palestinians remain fearful that the unilateral pull back could forestall a broader settlement, while many Israelis fear that, without a comprehensive agreement, the governing entity that will emerge in Gaza could be militant and threatening. Of course there are also the die-hard supporters of more and expanded settlements, who see no need for any concessions. Let us hope, this time, that the parties favoring reconciliation and ready to make compromises will persevere in spite of the potholes that will inevitably crop up along this road to peace.

Myth or Reality?

i. Arabs/Muslims Hate the US
for Its Affluence and Way of Life

In attempts to explain the seemingly growing conflict between the East and the West, blame is often placed at the doorstep of envy. Perhaps there may be a small element of truth in this allegation. Competition in the global marketplace and in the political arena can lead to feelings of superiority or deficiency, with predictable results. Many seem to hold the view that terror against the United States and its citizens, as well as Israel, is driven basically by envy. A more informed observer might, indeed, conclude that other peoples of this world may be impressed, maybe even awed, by Western affluence, its democratic systems, and its worldwide successes. But perhaps a reasonable case can be made that these peoples do not really aspire to a western way of life as they understand it. What in reality does the world know of, say, the American way of life? Yes, many Arabs and other Muslims have been educated in the US or Europe and some have settled in these places. These few do know Americans and Europeans for who they are today. Most others, however, receive their knowledge and form perceptions from what they see and hear in the media that so often seems to concentrate on the negative aspects of western society and culture. What tends to appear in western newspapers, magazines and books? What do our movies and television programs most often portray? What seems to dominate in these is extreme violence, fraud, explicit sex, broken laws, foul language or all of the above. Then they see the morality of some of our highest elected officials, scandals involving our lawmakers, fraud and greed in our largest corporations, depravity in some of our churches, and they see and hear things like the US Supreme Court rule that virtual pornography is just freedom of speech. These things do not properly characterize or define the American or European people, but it is not hard to see why the impression of an outsider, looking in, may be somewhat distorted. It may not be difficult to understand why our way of life here may not seem that attractive to the Muslim who is brought up in and taught extreme modesty, abstinence, honesty and reservation.

The world is falling out of love with us. Twenty or thirty years ago pretty much all things American or European were admired and emulated. People were taken with our low key manner, our taste in food, our clothing, our sports and just about everything else about us. No more. Even our very creative and entertaining TV shows are on the wane. In 2003 it was reported that American TV shows were losing much of their audience around the world. Shortly after 9/11 American foreign policy and influence was clearly becoming a source of contention not only among those suffering from those policies but also among those countries long considered close and dependable allies. Many I personally interviewed expressed a sense of relief that, at least on television, American culture was less a threat than it once was.

After 9/11 the world has become aware of the existence of the so-called "Madrassa". The word in Arabic means schools, but the madrassa, in the sense we have come to understand, is a very special kind of school that teaches a very puritanical form of Islam and a hatred of the West. Its proponents espouse a form of Islam that is totally intolerant and, at least in my experience, not really representative of mainstream Islamic thought. The madrassas have manipulated young minds and misused Islam for political purposes. The brainwashing of young kids to grow up with hatred of another people is not a common Islamic objective, yet it does exist and must be dealt with in no uncertain terms.

In the final analysis people and countries are judged by their actions. Establishing western military basis in other countries, most notably in the Middle East, is seen as intrusive and foreboding. The economic and military power and the international political influence of the West smacks as imposing, threatening and arrogant. It is particularly damaging when it is seen as supporting corrupt and non-representative local governments. We laud our own democratic principles and freedoms, yet western powers often support autocratic and unrepresentative regimes around the world in exchange for their support for the economic or military objectives of these powers. A fairly common view in many developing countries is that it is better to be ruled poorly by one of their own than to be ruled well by an outsider or one beholden to an outsider. There is a tendency to label a country as 'stable' if it facilitates our own regional interests, even when the leadership of that country may be repressive and dictatorial. Support for such regimes helps frustrate a participatory role for its citizens in their own welfare. They often lash out at America, but their target, more realistically, is their own corrupt government that is perpetuated because of America's support and tacit endorsement.

Such is the picture we paint for ourselves, and yet, too often, we profess an inability to understand why people may not love us. It hasn't always been this way. Perhaps we all can remember, not that many years ago, when the West was admired, respected and emulated virtually everywhere. In pursuit of what we perceive to be our own interest, maybe we are losing sight of the other guy, how our actions are affecting or have affected him or her. The West is advancing at a rapid pace and the internet and globalization are opening the eyes of the whole world to the freedoms and prosperity all around them. What was passively accepted in the past is now questioned. They ask, "Why should I stagnate and accept hurt while world powers pursue and achieve their own global interest in my backyard and at my expense?"

It is not our democracy that motivates people to hate us. It is not our liberty that turns students into human bombs. Maybe, just maybe, it is something that we have done, either directly or indirectly, either on purpose or inadvertently, that is denying other people the freedoms that we enjoy and hold dear, and are unattainable to them. I hope it is not wrong to explore this possibility, however unpopular or unpatriotic some try to make it seem.

ii. Israel's Right to the Holy Land Was:

1.   *Promised by God*
2.   *Ordained by the UN*
3.   *Won by Conquest*
4.   *Earned by Stewardship*

1. *A Promise of God*: In Genesis 12:7 the Bible says, "Then the Lord appeared to Abram (Abraham) and said, 'to your offspring I will give this land'." By 'land' the reference is to Canaan, which is more or less the land of Palestine. This promise is repeated again in Genesis 24:7 and in the New Testament Book of Romans. Now Abraham had two sons, the eldest, Ishmael, was conceived by Hagar, a maidservant. Initially unable to bear children, Sarah encouraged Abraham to father a child by Hagar. The second son, Isaac, Sarah's true son, was born later. There came a time when Sarah urged Abraham to banish Hagar and her son so that Ishmael would not inherit from Abraham. When Abraham hesitated, according to Genesis 21:12, the Lord appeared to him and said, "Listen to whatever Sarah tells you because it is through Isaac that your offspring will be reckoned. I will (also) make the son of the maidservant into a nation because he is your offspring." And then the son of Isaac, Jacob, after he had tricked his older brother out of his birthright, was promised the land of Canaan. (Genesis 28:13) So the Bible does indeed promise the land of Canaan to the descendants of the common patriarch of the Jews and the Arabs, with that promise flowing through the offspring of Jacob.

This promise was made some 3000 years before Israel was established as a sovereign nation. One might wonder if that promise was in fact fulfilled when King Saul, King David and King Solomon ruled the area between the 11th and 7th centuries BC, or between 145–63 BC when the Hasmoneans ruled Judah. Was the promise to be realized in 1948 or was it in fact realized much earlier, or perhaps to be realized at a later date?

The King-Crane Commission, sent by President Woodrow Wilson in 1919 to make recommendations on the future of Palestine, dismissed the Zionist historical claim to the Holy Land saying, "such a claim can hardly be considered."

It should also be mentioned here that the Palestinians are not new comers or immigrants to the area. They are the descendants of the Canaanites and the Philistines and have lived continuously on the land for over 2000 years. It's a pity that the Jews and the Arabs have been unable to share the land to which they both lay legitimate claim.

More fundamentally, one must carefully examine the full implication of reliance on historical and/or religious texts to justify the establishment of modern day political entities. It is hardly an approach commonly practiced. There are many Jews and Jewish organizations that are not at all supportive of the way Israel was created. According to their beliefs, the Jews were not to reclaim the Holy Land in conflict, but in peace. Their return was to have been coincident with the coming of the Messiah. If adopted universally the use of such religious references and ancient manuscripts to establish today's political boundaries and to create new nations would open up a veritable Pandora's Box, a whole new approach to geopolitics, requiring a re-demarcation in virtually every country.

For Believers, the Bible does provide a framework supportive of the Jewish claim to the land of Palestine, but the question remains whether such an approach to nation building has, or even should have, any legitimate international acceptance or validity.

2. *A Resolution of the United Nations*: It is true that the United Nations, in 1947, passed a resolution partitioning Palestine, awarding the Jewish homeland 56% of Palestine with Jerusalem to be administered by a separate international body. Notwithstanding this UN action, regrettably, the decision was far from universally accepted or legally attested. The basis by which an international body, such as the UN, could unilaterally award a portion of another country to an immigrant group to set up their own state within it, and against the will of the indigenous people remains an issue of debate.

3. *Spoils of War*: Acquisition of land by conquest is not an unheard of doctrine in history. There are many examples around the world where large tracts of land have been ceded by one country to another following a conflict. In 1945 peace loving nations of the world came together under the flag of the United Nations to introduce greater order and to promote peace and harmony among nations. Gains from military incursions are contrary to the spirit of the UN charter, which is to promote peace and harmony in the world. Moreover UN resolutions 242 and 338, endorsed also by the United States, required the Israelis and the Palestinians to return to pre-1967 borders.

It is also sometimes heard that the Palestinians fled, abandoning their homes and property, and hence somehow lost title to them, enabling or empowering the state of Israel to expropriate. According to several sources, both Arab and Jewish, Palestinians fled, not voluntarily but for fear of massacre at the hands of Jewish extremists, and then were barred from returning. An old Ottoman law, used by Israel to justify the expropriation of property from absentee Arab landowners, does not seem to enjoy a high degree of international validity.

4. *Rights of Stewardship*: Another claim sometimes heard implies that Israel has proved itself better able to develop the land and to create a modern state, and so, somehow, this entitles it to the land it now occupies or justifies occupation. Israel has indeed been very resourceful and successful in creating a modern and highly productive state. Impressive developments have occurred in technology, agriculture and manufacturing. But, here again, such a rationale for acquiring another's property does not enjoy popular or legal support. The ability of your neighbor to improve on your property cannot entitle him to share in it.

Israel exists and its status as a sovereign nation is actually pretty universally accepted by all Arab and Muslim states. Unfortunately, there is a hard core group from several quarters in the Arab world that opposes Israel's very existence. The longer the conflict remains unresolved, I fear the ranks of this group will swell. It is the obligation of every nation to subdue radical forces that work against the laws of the land and the best interest of the people. Every citizen of every nation is entitled to live in peace and tranquility. That dream is shared by Arab and Jew alike.

One might observe that Israel has not taken the opportunity of occupation to demonstrate all of the positive benefits to the Palestinians of a harmonious and peaceful working relationship with them. On the contrary what has been most apparent are oppressive measures such as curfews, school closings, work lockouts, confiscation of property, bulldozing of homes, uprooting of orchards, targeted assassinations, imprisonment, often for years and without charges—all in the name of improved security for Israel. There seems to have been few benefits such as the building of schools and hospitals and democratic institutions that might have been helpful in encouraging the Palestinians to become more responsible neighbors and building a more positive relationship between two peoples destined somehow to live together or to suffer together, in one fashion or another. This is certainly not who the Jews are as a people, but this is what has so often surfaced as the conflict keeps getting uglier, on both sides, and continues unresolved.

International, as well as Israeli, humanitarian organizations have condemned both Israel and the Palestinian leadership on many occasions for human rights violations. Aside from the annual reports of organizations such as Amnesty International and Bteselem, the subject has been highlighted frequently in newspaper articles. Human Rights Watch is the largest US-based human rights organization. In its 2003 Annual Report, released in January 2003, it criticized both the Israeli army and the armed Palestinian groups for a year that claimed more civilian lives but also highlighted the failure of the international community at large to effectively deal with abuses.

Aside from what is generally accepted as fair and just, the United Nations has a lot to say about treatment of people under occupation. While not specific to the Israeli occupation of the West bank and Gaza, as it predates those times, the general intent of Article 22 seems clear and applicable to any people under occupation:

"—There should be applied the principle that the well-being and development of such peoples (i.e. people from colonies and territories formally under Turkish rule) form a sacred trust of civilization and that securities for the performance of this trust should be embodied in this Covenant.—

Certain communities formerly belonging to the Turkish Empire have reached a stage of development where their existence as independent nations can be provisionally recognized subject to the rendering of administrative advice and assistance by a Mandatory until such time as they are able to stand alone. The wishes of these communities must be a principal consideration in the selection of the mandatory."

Further Article 73 of the UN Charter dealing with "Non Self-governing Territories" states:

"—The interests of the inhabitants of these territories are paramount, and accept as a sacred trust the obligation to promote to the utmost, within the system of international peace

and security established by the present Charter, the well-being of the inhabitants of these territories, and, to this end:

a. To ensure, with due respect for the culture of the peoples concerned, their political, economic, social, and educational advancement, their just treatment, and their protection against abuses;

b. To develop self-government, to take due account of the political aspirations of the peoples, and to assist them in the progressive development of their free political institutions, according to the particular circumstances of each territory and its peoples and their varying stages of advancement;

c. To further international peace and security;

d. To promote constructive measures of development, to encourage research, and to co-operate with one another and, when and where appropriate, with specialized international bodies with a view to the practical achievement of the social, economic, and scientific purposes set forth in this Article—"

As an example, it does not bode well that in early 2003 the Israeli Supreme Court dismissed a petition from the Palestinian Red Crescent and the Israeli Physicians for Human Rights that asked Israel to extend the distribution of gas masks to Palestinians in the occupied territories in the event of a gas attack by Iraq, in spite of its eight month reoccupation of the territories. The Israelis certainly deserve peace and protection from all forms of terrorism. It is owed security for its people. But it would seem, heretofore, that its policies for achieving that peace and security have been less than enlightened and quite often counterproductive. Somewhere there must be a line between counter terrorism and abuse of human rights.

On the other hand, one must again observe that Palestinian random attacks on unsuspecting Israeli civilians are not only despicable; they hinder support for the achievement of an internationally recognized Palestinian state.

iii. Islam Is a Religion of Violence

While by no means are all Muslims terrorists, it seems today that virtually all terrorists are Muslim.

In his book entitled *Bin Laden, Islam and America's War on Terrorism*, As'ad AbuKhalil posits, "When Muslims are accused of terrorism there is an impulse to study Islam, thereby drawing an association between Islam and terrorism. Muslims like others are driven by socioeconomic, political and cultural forces." Some right wing conservative Christian leaders have pronounced that Muslims and Christians do not worship the same God. For peoples that believe in only one god that seems to be a rather fallacious statement. Muslims, Jews and Christians all share belief in much of the Old Testament scriptures. Muslims believe in virtually all the Old Testament prophets and that Mohammed was the last of the prophets. Muslims even believe in the virgin birth of Jesus, and in the Koran there are miracles accorded to Jesus that do not appear in the Bible. They believe that the Bible was corrupted by its adherents and a new revelation, the revelation of Mohammed, was sent from God. Bernard Lewis, the highly respected Middle Eastern historian, notes that the Muslims believe that Judaism and Christianity were both 'true' religions in their time. Their essential truths are incorporated in the Koran which, for the Muslim world, has now superseded all other scriptures. Surah II, verse 62 says, "Surely those who believe, and those who are Jews, and the Christians, and the Sabians (also known as Christians of St. John, Nasoraeans and Subbi), whoever believe in Allah and the last day and does good, they shall have their reward from their Lord, and there is no fear for them, nor shall they grieve."

The view of Islam as a religion has been distorted by the actions of the radical fringes, and the Muslim mainstream, regrettably, remains characteristically silent. To many, Muslims are all cut from the same cloth and exhibit the same kind of behavior. This is a misconception and an unfair characterization and stereotyping. There is a brotherhood between Muslims that is generally more pervasive than loyalty to a political entity. And there is probably no more special disposition to violence in the Koran than in the Bible. In Islam starting a war is immoral. Surah VIII, verse 61 states "And if they incline to peace, then incline to it." Surah XIII, verse 40 makes it clear that Muslims are to be messengers to others (the unbelievers), but not enforcers: "—for only the delivery of the message is incumbent upon you, while calling them to account is Ours (God's business)". Bernard Lewis asserts that suicide bombers are forbidden in Islam in no uncertain terms.

Admittedly, there have been many abuses in history but these are generally perpetrated by that radical fringe element. We still have vivid memories of Arabs dancing in the streets after the 9/11 disaster. Behavior that applauds loss of innocent life can only be deplored. While not wanting to be an apologist, I do know the Arab mind well enough perhaps to see a different message in that celebration. Firstly, Arabs traditionally believe in the strongest family and personal ties and life is no less important to them as it is to us in the West. Secondly, while, no doubt, there are many exceptions I really don't believe that Arabs who have been on the receiving end of so much suffering and grief at the hands of the West for so long can see joy in the suffering of other innocent people. The outpouring of sympathy and condolences received after 9/11 from many

Muslim sources, some I personally witnessed, is a testament to that. Rather, it is somewhat like us on August 14th 1945, V.J. (Victory in Japan) Day, when we all took to the streets in jubilation. We were not celebrating the loss of 132,000 Japanese civilians in Hiroshima and Nagasaki a few days before; we were celebrating the defeat of Japan. In a similar fashion perhaps the Arabs dancing in the street were celebrating the shifting of the battle from their homeland (for a change) into the heart of America who was then and is still today perceived, if not their direct enemy, at least the 'enabler' of their misery. To many, the Middle East has been the battleground for Western interests too many times; it somehow seemed right to them that this conflict be at least shared with the principal proponents. But perhaps such is the consequence of war and misery that allows the worst in people to emerge. It is irresponsible and thoughtless behavior that tends to reinforce in the minds of people a propensity to violence in the psyche of the Muslim.

Yet Muslims have become enraged with what they perceive as double standards. Calls are made to Muslims to free themselves from the influence of terrorists but there is no such appeal to the Pope or to the Protestant community to free their religions from the influence of terrorism when people of their sects commit acts of violence, like the Oklahoma City bombing of the Federal Building in 1995, killing 168 people, or the later bombing of abortion clinics, just to name two incidents. It is true that the offenders have been apprehended, tried, found guilty and punished but no stigmatism has been attached to their religions. Of course the chief difference can be attributed to radical Muslim clerics that might take it upon themselves to proclaim a message of violence, revenge and jihad from the pulpit of mosques. It is not surprising that an association between violence and the Islamic faith is presumed. The large, dissenting majority of devout Muslim and learned imams who remain quiet are the chief culprits in this perception for not speaking out more vociferously and emphatically. In Islam there is no 'Pope' and no one spokesperson. There is no single overriding authority to ensure that a consistent, uniform and agreed message is conveyed to the world. Every cleric can voice his own views from the pulpit of his mosque, and those that speak the loudest seem to attract the most attention.

Fareed Zakaria in his book *"The Future of Freedom"* suggests that the rise of Islamic fundamentalism is caused by the total failure of political institutions in the Arab world. The Fundamentalist call in Arab lands has resonance because it invites men to participate—in contrast to their political culture that reduces citizens to spectators. As'ad AbuKhalil, in his book, notes that fundamentalists in all religions are quite similar in outlook and objectives. They all tend to be intolerant, puritanical, often armed, willing to use force and ready to die.

iv. A Country Has the Right to Preemptively Attack Other Sovereign Nations and to Carry Out Selective Assassinations of Suspected Terrorist When Its Security Is Threatened

The right of every country to protect its citizens and its legitimate interests is sacrosanct. However, when the achievement of that goal involves encroachment on the sovereign rights of other states and the personal rights of other people, then one must tread carefully. The West has been hesitant to criticize Israeli encroachments into the West Bank and Gaza when it believes Israeli security is threatened. The invasion of Iraq in 2003 by the United States and its coalition partners has elevated to a new level the debate on pre-emptive attacks. Are preemptive attacks a just and legitimate course of self defense? Are security and the right to peace and tranquility of equal importance to all peoples? In the pursuit of suspected or possibly would-be terrorists, is 'collateral damage', that is, loss of other innocent life and property, however regrettable, an acceptable consequence? Where is the line between counter-terrorism and abuse of human rights? It would seem that widespread acceptance of such a pre-emption principle would set a new and rather dangerous precedent that would threaten world order and stability. The Palestinian-Israeli experience seems to confirm that, in today's high-tech world, barriers, buffer zones, targeted assassinations, military incursions and rigid controls cannot guarantee lasting security. Yes, these can be a short term deterrent but they do not produce long term peace. Peace is only possible when both parties to the conflict desperately want a harmonious relationship. What has been happening in the Middle East over the last few years has decidedly not advanced the cause of peace. The policies of both parties are counter-productive.

The targeting of innocent Israelis by Palestinian extremist groups does not advance the Palestinian cause nor contribute to the recovery of their lands. Israeli incursions into Arab lands, targeted assassinations and destruction of Arab property do not enhance Israel's aspiration for long term peace and security. After 39 years one would think that observation obvious. Apparently it is not.

The world has been cautious in its criticism of Israel for fear of being accused of anti-Semitism. In his book, *The Holocaust Industry*, Norman Finkelstein—whose parents were survivors of the Nazi death camps—noted, "evoking historic persecution (the holocaust) deflects present day criticism."

However, persistence in a wrong does not transform that wrong into a right. Someone once said that decisions on war are in the hands of the Arabs and Jews, but decisions on peace are in the hands of those that give aid and comfort to these parties. In this the United States has a significant obligation and a unique opportunity. The world must find a way to ensure Israel's security while, at the same time, protecting the basic rights of the Palestinians. Life, security and happiness are pursuits of equal value to all peoples. A just and lasting solution to the Middle East conflict will never be achieved unless and until this is recognized and steps are taken to provide a quality life to the inhabitants on all sides and to afford all peoples an opportunity to participate in their own destiny.

v. Arab Governments Are Doing the Best They Can with Limited Capability

There are 22 Arab nations or political entities (including the Palestinians.) Their combined populations total nearly 300 million—bigger than the United States, yet their combined GDP is less than half that of the State of California. They have fallen behind the rest of the world by virtually every measure. Bernard Lewis correctly points out that they have lost out on the battlefield, at the marketplace and in the classroom. According to a recent UN sponsored study, today Arab countries average some 18 computers per 1000 persons, compared to 78 globally. All together they translate fewer books than Greece. They can boast only 371 scientist and engineers per one million persons compared to 979 globally. And this from a people who were once the acknowledged leaders in many scientific and academic fields, and once the foremost civilization in the world. What happened? Frustration with opportunities at home is inducing large numbers of the skilled and educated to immigrate to more promising and less dangerous places. Between 1995 and 1996, 25% of all BA graduates from Arab Universities emigrated from Arab lands. From 1998 to 2000 over 15,000 medical doctors left the Arab world.

Of the twenty two Arab entities, in only one did the leadership ascend to power in a free, open and internationally monitored election by the people. That one exception happened to be Yasser Arafat who was later marginalized for his alleged corruption and inability to curb terror attacks on Israel. In the others too often the political system seems to be one of cronyism, outright autocracy or inherited dynasty. The people have little voice in their own governments, let alone their own futures, and must accept with gratitude whatever is handed down to them.

Lebanon may be somewhat of an exception, but for the last 29 years has been under the umbrella of influence of Syria who, until just recently, maintained a sizable military and intelligence presence in the country to ensure its effective political and economic control. That control has finally been weakened, but probably not totally eliminated, following widespread public outcry in the aftermath of the assassination of former Prime Minister, Rafik Hariri, in February 2005 that led to international pressure for the Syrians to withdraw.

Those countries with oil wealth have a compounded problem. States with such immense natural resources have no need to burden the people with taxes. On the contrary, the government typically showers a part of these blessings on the people gratis. With the people making no contributions of any kind to the government what voice can they claim in the affairs of state? And requiring nothing from the people the government may reason that they owe them little. There is no accountability, no reckoning, and no voice. One of the appeals of Fundamentalism is that it invites adherents to participate, to be a contributing part of something, when they are excluded from any such participation by their own governments.

In most Arab countries the people are rarely empowered and women are intentionally excluded from the opportunity to be full contributing members of a progressive society, even though many are educated and skilled. Access to the outside world is often discouraged if not banned. Educational systems have fallen behind the rest of the world. And, worst of all, these ills are typically laid on the doorstep of outside powers. Few governments take responsibility for their own short-comings and little seems to be done to curtail rampant corruption that is siphoning off resources badly needed for internal development. The Arabs see themselves as victims of world powers who have exploited them for centuries. It is a fact that many injustices, indeed, have been dealt the Arab world, many promises broken and expectations shattered. Many of these non-representative regimes were established under the auspices of an allied power. In many instances good things came from the early colonial hegemony, but the legacy is not well remembered. Rightly or wrongly, the Arabs tend to blame others for the poor governments and repressive regimes under which they now live. In some of the countries in the Middle East the sense of tribalism is still very strong and allegiance is to the tribe first and to the state a distant second, particularly a state set up by outside forces. There is a strong common bond between tribal members. A tribe is often self-contained, being an economic unit, a social support structure, a system of justice, and a functioning alternative to a state.

One cannot view Arab resistance to the occupation of Palestinian lands as being particularly productive or effectual.

Starting from the poorly conceived, poorly coordinated and poorly executed military assistance to the Palestinians in the 1948 war, Arab efforts have fallen far short of achieving any notable objective. An exception might be the Arab boycott of Israeli products and services. Without endorsing such actions, one must acknowledge that denying Israel access to its natural contiguous markets has had a measurable negative impact on the Israeli economy. On the flip side, by forgoing trade with Israel, the nearby Arab economies no doubt have also suffered, both economically and politically. Aside from this the Arab governments have seemed powerless to produce a reasonable and unified position that would contribute to a peaceful resolution to the unending conflict with Israel. On the contrary, an observer might conclude that they have typically adopted strategies that were doomed to fail. There was a flicker of hope in April 2002 when the Arab league met in Beirut and the so-called Saudi Peace Plan was unveiled. Endorsed by all 22 members of the Arab League, this was the first time a well thought out and responsible proposal was advanced by the Arabs and presented to the world. Regrettably, to date, no action has been taken on this proposal by anyone. Arab leadership too often has been self-serving, incoherent and unrepresentative. Nevertheless, the Palestinian struggle has been and remains a popular issue to espouse for Arabs and most Muslim countries. One wonders to what extent this celebrated cause has helped divert attention from their own failed internal policies!

. In an editorial on the front page of one of Lebanon's newspapers in 2003, the author deplored Arab silence in the worldwide protests then taking place against the imminent war in Iraq. Whereas ten million people in the streets of hundreds of cities around the world demonstrated for peace, for the most part, Arab cities were empty. Aside from Beirut, where diverse political groups came together to denounce both the impending war and Saddam Hussein, there were few rational voices heard in Arab capitals. The editorial accused Arab leaders, not ostriches, of hiding their heads in the sand.

Since the occupation of the West Bank and Gaza in 1967, several Palestinian resistance groups have emerged. Hamas, an acronym for Islamic Resistance Movement, was formed in 1987 at the onset of the first 'Intifada' or popular uprising against Israeli occupation and has been the most active of these groups. In addition to their 'operations' against Israeli targets, they have provided needed social, medical and educational services to needy Palestinians and have thereby acquired a degree of legitimacy in the eyes of the local population and enjoy a good deal of sympathy and support. This is confirmed by their overwhelming success in the January 2006 parliamentary elections when they gained 74 out of 132 seats. However, one must conclude that their attacks on civilian targets have undermined their objective, detracted from their true mission and lost external support they might have otherwise enjoyed. Their recent participation in Palestinian elections is a welcomed sign. History records many instances when participation in a democratic process and the assumption of positions of national importance have brought about a broader, more mature and constructive demeanor. Let's hope such transformation is in the making as we speak.

Though not Palestinian, Hezbollah deserves mention since it has been the beneficiary of considerable attention, or rather, notoriety. This group, predominantly Lebanese Shiite supported by Iran and Syria, has had one overriding objective—to free Lebanon of foreign domination. It is said that this group is implicated in the suicide bombings of a US

Marine barracks as well as the French military garrison in Beirut in 1983. Later they conducted guerilla actions against the Israeli presence and control in the so-called buffer zone established by Israel in 1985 in the southern part of Lebanon. They were instrumental in finally forcing the withdrawal of Israeli troops in the year 2000. Since then Hezbollah has administered the southern part of Lebanon with a good deal of skill, and praise from the local population. They have also continued to be an irritant to Israel, lobbing rockets into northern Israeli villages from time to time. Hezbollah is accused of aiding Hamas and perhaps other confrontation groups in the region, an assertion I can neither confirm nor refute. They too are evolving into a credible political entity with aspirations for a more active role in government.

Arab shortcomings have not been confined to the Palestinian conflict. As the world all around the Middle East progresses, the Arab nations and many Islamic countries remain pretty much stagnant and mired in ancient traditions and practices that stifle advancement. The failing of the Arab is one of abandonment, the ability and willingness to accept the status quo, whatever the cost. Few risk demanding their rights, a voice in the affairs of state or a role in their own futures. When this changes, and one day it must, it may trigger internal upheaval and turmoil, but they will, at long last, be firmly on the road to revitalization, and the people will be able to aspire to a rightful place in the world among free and contributing members of a global society.

Admittedly in several Arab countries, including the Arab Emirates and Saudi Arabia, there have been some recent "baby-steps" taken to involve local citizens, and particularly women, in various legislative or municipal bodies, albeit with rather limited powers, or in chambers of commerce. In their defense for the long delays in this opening they will point out that it was not until 1920, 144 years after our declaration of independence, that American women were granted the right to vote. So they see their progress as acceptable. It is this sense of rationalization that impedes recognition that it is not the rate of improvement that is relevant or important, but rather the position they command today relative to the competing globalized forces in the world.

vi. Crushing the PLO and Other Extremist Will Eliminate Terrorism

History does not always support the notion that suppression will render a people docile. This certainly has not been the experience in Palestine. Prime Minister Sharon's incursions into the West Bank in the spring of 2002 to suppress Palestinian terror attacks and suicide bombings reeked havoc in many West Bank towns and villages and killed hundreds of Palestinians, but it is hard to conclude that this action eliminated, or even significantly reduced, potential terrorism. The same observation may be made of the incursions into Gaza in the fall of 2004. More often than not, devastation and depravation seem to create a breeding ground for more terrorists. It is against human nature to assume that people are born evil or born with a death wish. People from around the world all seem to start out pretty much the same but eventually become products of their own environments. While no doubt exceptions always exist, by and large, a happy, supportive and participatory environment tends to foster progressive, law-abiding people. Conversely, people born and raised with strife, suppression and hopelessness tend to resort to desperate acts. It is no surprise that Palestinian refugee camps are a fertile recruitment ground for future 'martyrs'.

The West views acts of terrorism with total outrage and that is a normal and an accepted reaction. All forms of terrorism must be condemned. But what is condemnation but mere words? Condemnation does not eliminate terrorism. More than just words, more than condemnation and more than reactive violence are required to combat terrorism. Terrorism is rarely an end unto itself but a tactic to achieve some political, social or religious objective. However, if left unaddressed, destruction of the perceived enemy survives and replaces the initial goal and becomes the ongoing raison d'etre.

In our so-called "war on terror" there is a misconception that probably leads us to erroneous conclusions. Wars are declared on enemies which are states, countries or political entities or maybe organized gangs. "Terror" is an instrument, or a weapon, chosen to wield against a foe. To declare war on "terror" is like declaring war on the B52 strategic bomber or the atom bomb. Throughout history terror has been used to further the goals of national, political, religious or social groups. The legitimate object of our war is not terror per se; it is the injustice or misconceptions that lead people to resort to this form of manifestation, demonstration and reaction.

At some point, however unpopular it might be post 9/11, the world community of nations must ask what it has done to induce people to kill themselves to bring harm to its citizens and to its establishments. It is important to observe that many of the terrorists are not poor, deprived and uneducated desperados. Quite often they are well educated, well traveled and well off. They are idealists who have taken it upon themselves to fight for a principal, to rectify an injustice or to salvage Muslim, Arab or family honor. Others successfully exploit the misery of many of their compatriots who have little to lose in martyrdom. Studies carried out on terrorists have concluded that many eagerly seek martyrdom, an act that transforms their disconsolation into glory, defeat into triumph and anonymity into public adulation.

In the final analysis it might be unreasonable to ask people who have reached the depths of desperation and despair to behave according to someone else's norms. At some point the root of the problem must be uncovered and dealt with.

vii. Terrorism Is a Legitimate Weapon of Resistance and War

Terrorism is defined as the systematic use of terror, or fear, as a means of coercion. The real object of terrorism is rarely just to kill people, but rather to instill anxiety, to disrupt routine and to create panic. There is no doubt that in many instances in the annals of history terrorism has been an instrument used to obtain a particular objective, be it political or otherwise. This does not make it justifiable, but it has been frequently used and one would also have to admit that the use of terror tactics has often been effective. Does the end justify the means? That has been a question debated throughout history; a question for which there is not a universally agreed answer. Moreover, the answer may not always be obvious nor is it necessarily the same in every case. Coming out of 9/11 there was zero tolerance in America for anything that smacks of terrorism. Any attack on innocent civilians is an act to be vehemently denounced and requires immediate and unqualified retaliation. The Palestinian extremists groups totally misjudged this.

This book is an effort, an attempt, to understand the Middle East conflict and the Middle East mind. To do this it may be helpful to try and see the issue from the perspective of each of the parties to the conflict. I am assuming a license I have not been granted in presenting the two sides, but perhaps they are perspectives that are not all that far off. We will view the minority extremist position on both sides, since it is they who are driving the conflict. The 'silent' majority tends to be the moderates who, left to their own devices, might well be able to hammer out a compromise acceptable to both sides. It is always the few extremists that keep the pot boiling. Regrettably, it is often these high profile fringe groups that drive the agenda.

From the extremist Israeli position—"Our presence in the Holy Land was promised to Abraham by God and has been sanctioned and endorsed by the United Nations. For what we suffered before and during World War II, the world owes us not only our own state, but also security and tranquility and support for our actions. We were persecuted throughout Europe. We were corralled like cattle, labeled, stripped of our possessions, torn away from our families and sent off to labor camps or to extermination centers. Our attempts to assimilate into other communities were rejected. We had no place to turn except to the land of our roots. Our occupation of the West Bank and Gaza are legitimate spoils of war resulting from the defensive initiative we took when we were threatened by our neighbors. Innocent civilians, women and children, have been brutally murdered in restaurants, in shopping malls and on buses. Acts of terror result in loss of innocent life, induce fear and uncertainty in our people and devastates our economy. It is therefore imperative that the world respect our right to exist and that acts of violence against us cease. Any measure, any measure at all, we take that ensures our security must be good enough to others. Moreover, the Palestinian terrorists are a part of a worldwide network directed against western civilization. Our confrontation therefore aids in that broader fight against this terror threat."

From the extremist Palestinian position—"What the world chooses to call terrorism, we call legitimate resistance to military occupation and exploitation of our land. Today there is virtually no other civilized country in the world that occupies another's land, and the West has not only tolerated this in our case but has also, through its actions or inactions, supported the Israeli occupation. We have no tanks or airplanes with which to resist the fourth most powerful military in the world. We have only our bodies. In most wars, people who sacrifice their lives for a just cause are called heroes; we are called murderers. It's all so unfair. We cannot go against the Israeli army; we can only go against soft targets that include civilians. We have no other way to pursue our resistance. Israeli soldiers routinely kill our civilians with rare protests from the international community. And the Palestinians did not invent attacks on civilian targets. What about the IRA in Northern Ireland, the Mau Mau rebellion in Kenya against the British, the Algerian uprising against the French—just to name a few. And what about your own Samson who brought down the temple on himself and those who persecuted him, including women and children. Was Samson a terrorist, a suicide bomber? What about the acts of the Stern and Irgun gangs active during the struggle for an Israeli state, the massacre at Deir Yassin, killing 254 men, women and children, the blowing up of the King David Hotel, killing 92, the assassination of the UN mediator, Count Bernadotte? Leaders of some of these gangs became respected heads of states and heroes commemorated on postage stamps. (And then they hit us where it really hurts.) They ask what about the two atomic bombs you Americans dropped on Japan in 1945 to end World War II, killing 132,000 civilians? Was that not terrorism? There seems to be a standard for the Palestinians and a different standard for the rest of the world. If you want to eliminate terrorism, just leave our land. In the final analysis to halt our resistance is to accept Israeli occupation, and we can never abandon our struggle so long as the injustice remains. For most of the world Hamas, Islamic Jihad and Al-Aqsa Brigade are just terrorist organizations bent on killing innocent people, but for us they are nationalist resistance organizations, much like the Jewish Stern and Irgun gangs in pre-Israel days, driven to violent acts by their oppressors."

What is it that causes people to violate the teachings of their own religions and wreak atrocities on their adversaries, whether it is the bombing of an Israeli bus carrying innocent women and children, or whether it is the machine gunning of Muslim worshipers as they pray in a mosque? There can be no doubt that both Israelis and Palestinians must be allowed to live in peace and to be secure within their own borders. The question becomes how can both aims be realized? What solution is both just and achievable? Maybe justice is as simple as a return to the pre-1967 borders. But is that achievable? The record to date is not encouraging.

viii. Solving the Palestinian/Israeli Conflict Will Eliminate Islamic Terrorism

That would be nice but, lamentably, wishful thinking. Terrorism takes at least two forms. The first I would call "Resistance" terrorism. The Palestinian and the Chechnyan struggles, where peoples are striving to reverse an imposed situation they deem unfair or unjust, are examples of this. This is not to condone their actions but only to say theirs is a specific and limited objective. In both of the above cases it is decidedly not a religious struggle. The Chechnyan Muslims are not waging war against the Christian Russians. Rightly or wrongly they are waging a political war for national independence from Russia. Likewise, the Palestinian/Israeli conflict is not about Islam against Judaism. It is Palestinians, who are largely Muslim but include a sizable Christian minority, against the state of Israel who they see illegally occupying their land and suppressing their freedoms. A satisfactory solution to these conflicts should indeed eliminate terrorism from these sources. Of course there will always be elements that can never be satisfied with any outcome, that can never forget or forgive the wrongs done to them and will continue their 'resistance'. Hopefully, they would be a minor group with little indigenous support, and therefore controllable.

There is a fine line between 'resistance' and "terrorism' and it seems quite easy to spill over from one to the other. What is often considered legitimate resistance sometimes impacts innocents who are not parties to the conflict; they are not the target. On the other hand terrorism often specifically targets civilians. It would not be unreasonable to expect, or at least to hope, that in today's 'civilized' world it would be possible to resolve conflicts and injustices without resorting to any form of violence. That remains a seemingly illusive goal and is perhaps an indictment of our international organizations and leadership.

The second group of terrorist is more worrisome, for whereas they may have started off with a list of real, or maybe imagined, grievances, their real issue eventually is transformed to one of power, control and perhaps wealth. Their leaders tend to be shrewd, ruthless and very persuasive. In the name of some popular cause they are able to elicit a following ready and willing to do their dastardly bidding, even to the death. They tend to be charismatic, well organized and relentless. Perhaps an example would be Adolph Hitler during World War II, who was able to induce a noble nation to follow him into a war of aggression and ultimately to commit horrible acts of barbarity on humanity. Another example may be Osama Bin Laden, sometimes labeled the 'mother' of all terrorist, who has been able to create a tight knit, well financed, worldwide network of committed followers. It is unclear, and we may never know, if the grievances on Ben Laden's list, and they are well documented, are all resolved that he would cease and desist from all terror activities. I don't know the answer but it would seem that many of his followers and many of the copycat groups that have surfaced may well search for other causes to justify their continued terror actions. Osama and his lieutenants have been able to marshal the support and blind dedication not only from desolate and oppressed people but also from others, more educated and affluent, who have bought into his grand scheme of rejection. Many such disgruntled terror groups while not necessarily espousing the same goal, find common cause in resisting a common enemy, and readily collaborate in the havoc they peddle. Examples of this have surfaced in Iraq where many of the insurgents are foreigners whose presence there has little to do with Iraq and much to do with broader, unpopular US policies in the region. In a very real sense many adherents find the power, the glory and the notoriety sufficient motivation for their acts of terror; the ultimate goal becomes a secondary consideration. Such terrorists will probably always be terrorists. No promise, no accommodation and no settlement will appease their zeal for violent acts. For many of the volunteer suicide bombers, the choice between their current dead-end lives and the glorious notoriety of a spectacular death, and all the publicity that goes with it, is an easy one. Factor in the promises of great rewards in paradise and you have a long ready pool of duped candidates. Some no doubt volunteer for these one way missions for personal reasons, to avenge a death or some terrible wrong that has been inflicted on them or their families, maybe sweetened by a financial reward to a destitute family. For all those in this group the only alternative available, the only effective course of action, is deliberate and decisive counter force.

At the same time, it is mandatory that legitimate grievances and injustices—and there are many—be addressed with great urgency lest they continue to fester, enriching the breeding ground for future terrorists.

The Solution?

It would seem the question today is not 'what is the solution?' but, indeed, is a lasting solution possible? After nearly thirty-nine years it is fairly obvious that neither the parties themselves nor the international community of nations have been able to arrive at a comprehensive, workable plan leading to real and lasting peace. The "Road Map" perhaps does offer some hope, not so much because of its content, but because of the dedication of the external powers to a solution. Up until recently what seemed clear was that the leadership on both sides was tainted with failure and had lost both the credibility and the capability or will to arrive at a just and lasting resolution. Today, with Israel's withdrawal from Gaza and with new leadership in the post-Arafat, post-Sharon era, perhaps there can once again be renewed hope. A resolution that will stand the test of time cannot be based on what one or the other might be forced to accept at a given moment, but on what is fundamentally just. Someone once said that for too long the problem on the Palestinian side was there was no one to talk to, and on the Israeli side no one to listen. Some might say that the UN created this problem and now it must resolve it. Just as the partition of Palestine was imposed on the parties by the United Nations, perhaps another externally generated plan, like the Road Map, should be likewise imposed. To succeed such a solution would have to have the full weight and commitment of the United Nations, and most specifically the United States, behind it. Various suggestions have been put forth by think tanks and academicians. While professing neither great insight nor rare wisdom, it would seem that the key elements of any lasting solution should include:

1.) A return to pre-1967 borders with certain equitable land swaps based on demographics.
2.) The creation and recognition of a Palestinian sovereign state in the West Bank, Gaza and East Jerusalem.
3.) Establishment of Jerusalem as joint capitals, again with division based on demographics.
4.) The dismantling of all settlements falling within the Palestinian areas.
5.) Security guarantees for both states, monitored for an initial period by international observers.
6.) Settling of the refugee issue either by compensation or resettlement in the newly established Palestine, not into Israel.
7.) Resolution of control over natural resources and air space.
8.) Financial and administrative assistance to the Palestinian state to aid in the establishment of democratic institutions and a viable governmental entity.
9.) Demilitarization of the Palestinian state for an agreed period of time.
10.) The establishment of trade, educational and cultural exchanges between Israel and Palestine.
11.) Perhaps a Palestinian defense and economic treaty with Jordan.

The most critical need is time to heal the wounds between the two peoples, to re-establish trust and respect and harmony. It is relatively easy to rebuild homes and repave roads. To rebuild a family that has been devastated in some way requires an element of human character and forgiveness that only time can accommodate. The longer the battle rages the longer the period of convalescence.

Any solution will require serious compromises from both parties. Tough compromises will never be accepted universally but must have the support of a substantial majority of the people. Such consensus cannot be obtained without strong, enlightened leadership. Today there is turmoil on both sides of the Israeli-Palestinian border. The Palestinians have two competing political entities with different agendas. The more moderate Fatah movement with its leader, Mahmoud Abbas, the current president of the Palestinian Authority does not enjoy the support of the more fundamentalist Hamas movement which has begun solidifying its transition from a resistance group to a more broadly defined political bloc. There are various other groups, labeled by most as terrorist, which are a part of the Palestinian landscape and which are against any form of settlement. The onus is on the Palestinians to put their house in order and to speak with one unified voice. Arriving at such an accommodation could be painful and it could take time. Regretfully time is not their friend.

On the Israeli side, over the last few years Prime Minister Sharon evolved from an aggressive military commander and adamant supporter of settlement expansion to something of a realistic peace-pursuing diplomat. His unilateral withdrawal from Gaza and plans to withdraw from several West Bank settlements were gutsy moves which placed him at odds with a good many members of his own Likud party. This internal conflict led him to withdraw from Likud and form yet another political party, Kadima, dedicated to forging peace with its neighbors. But Sharon is now succeeded by leadership with yet untested skills in consensus building and peacemaking. It seems incumbent on the Israelis to get behind their leader and accept the hard choices that confront them for the higher reward of peace and tranquility.

There will always be elements within both societies who will strive to undermine any compromises that will lead to a lasting solution. For diehard terrorist groups or disgruntled nationalists to quickly abandon their struggle is probably unlikely. Individuals who become terrorists have a propensity to die as terrorists. It will be incumbent on the new emerging states to establish and enforce the rule of law and to relentlessly pursue dissidents who refuse to accept the legitimacy of the peace accords and the resulting sovereignty of the states created.

Concluding Remarks

There is probably but one question that needs to be asked. At what price peace? Someone once said that love is not measured by what one gives but by what one is willing to give up. Similarly, what are the parties prepared to give up to achieve peace, stability and security? Inevitably it is not justice but power that determines the outcome of conflicts. It is the weakest party, not the party in the wrong that must make the most concessions. But peace on such basis is always temporary. When the wheel turns the wound will be reopened and old scores settled. It is only a win-win solution that survives the test of time.

The Palestinians have nothing tangible with which to negotiate. All of the discussions about peace and the creation of a Palestinian state hinge on what the Palestinians are willing to give up. Will they renounce the use of violence? How much of their claim to East Jerusalem will they abandon? How much of the remaining territories will they turn over to Israel? How many settlements on Arab land will they have to accommodate. How much sovereignty will they have to surrender? Everything that is up for grabs seems to be on the Palestinian side of the border. Israel, from its position of strength, must ask itself what it is prepared to give up in exchange for peace. To assume that an unjust settlement will end violence is, regrettably, wishful thinking. Does Israel want Palestinian land more than Israeli security? Does it want expansion of its borders or peace with its neighbors? It is really Israel's decision, not the Arabs. To date history has shown that the Palestinians will not accept the status quo. Israeli actions in the occupied territories in pursuit of terrorist, particularly since the early 2000 uprising, has not enhanced Israel's long term security. It may have reduced the number of suicide attacks for a while. It may have eliminated hundreds of terrorist, but in the process it has created a breeding ground for thousands. It has not broken the will of the Palestinians to resist occupation; it has intensified their determination to do so to the point where human life on either side has lost its value. It is the Samson syndrome.

To aspire to peace and security is not only just, it is a God given right. But the use of settlements, security fences and occupation as instruments to achieve these goals is indeed curious and demonstrably ineffective, certainly as a long range solution.

It is incumbent on the Palestinians to take charge of their own destiny and to demonstrate that they will not tolerate leadership that is corrupt and does not work tirelessly in their best interests. Regrettably, this is a problem rife in the Middle East. Yet insistence by Israel and the United States that they would no longer deal with Yasser Arafat, who was elected by the Palestinian people in 1988, only reinforced his legitimacy with his own people, who resented outside powers deciding who should or should not represent them. The same mistake may be occurring now with the international community refusing to deal with the Hamas government. The message which is being telegraphed is that democracy is wonderful but will be tolerated only if outside powers like the results. One can only hope that this or any other new administration will become an effective force, exerting responsible governmental leadership, pursuing peace with its neighbors and acting both independently and decisively to meet the great expectations of its people. It won't be easy.

Sometimes world leaders act just like kids. "You go first!" "No, you go first!" "You stop the violence and I'll withdraw."

"No, you withdraw and I'll stop the violence." Meanwhile more innocent people on both sides die. It seems more important to control the process or dictate the terms than to secure an acceptable outcome. Regrettably, compromises for the mutual good often only occur after the parties have totally exhausted or devastated one another. What is called for is the courageous, farsighted soul who will say, "I'll take a chance. I'll take the first step. If it works, great! If it doesn't, then I still have my options." Prime Minister Sharon's 2004 initiative to unilaterally withdraw from Gaza could be one such step provided it does not become an end in itself. This has presented an opportunity for both sides to demonstrate leadership and statesmanship. If the newly elected Hamas government can rapidly evolve into a responsible and non-belligerent administration, and if the Israeli unilateral withdrawal can be followed by real Palestinian autonomy in Gaza and if all this does not impede or slow down final peace negotiations for all the occupied territories, then there could, finally, be cause for optimism about the future. That would indeed be a historic achievement.

Today Israel is strong enough to maintain the status quo if it wishes. But in the years ahead it will no doubt find its neighbors growing stronger, more numerous and more menacing. Without a fair and just settlement today, tomorrow's clouds over the horizon could be darker, the situation more ominous. The road to peace starts and stops in Tel Aviv. The Israelis are powerful enough, smart enough, and I believe magnanimous enough to take the necessary unilateral steps, and without help from outside powers, to secure for itself and the region that peace and stability that has so long eluded the area. My hope, the hope of the civilized world, is that they will conclude that the solution is indeed simple and yet so rewarding.

A peace agreement between the Arabs and Israel is not the end of the story. For there to be real and lasting peace and prosperity in the region, the Israeli's have to be satisfied with what they have, and the Arabs have to finally take their place as valued and contributing members in the community of nations by putting their own houses in order. There must be internal changes, the unleashing of the potential of all the people through education and full and equal representation. Thomas Friedman in an op-ed piece stated the importance very succinctly. He quoted an old Indian proverb that says if we don't turn around we may just get to where we're headed. When nations, aspiring for progress and development, decide to change course, to stop blaming everybody else for their problems and to begin the process of internal renovation, not just of their infrastructure but, more importantly, of their attitudes, of their tolerance and acceptance of others and their perspectives on human behavior, they will, indeed, be on the right road. The good news is all this is possible without compromising their own values, culture or religion. All it takes is selfless determination. Regrettably, too often that is a tall order.

I have used the word "regrettably" 22 times in this book. I hope it was too much.

References:

The following selected references were consulted by the Author and provide useful information and perspective:

Albert Hourani, *A History of the Arab Peoples*, New York, MJF Books, 1991.
World Book Encyclopedia, 1979.
Microsoft Encarta Encyclopedia, 2003.
Alfred M. Lilienthal, *The Zionist Connection*, New York, Dodd, Mead & Company, 1978.
Mitchell Bard, *The Complete Idiots Guide to the Middle East Conflict*, Alpha Books, 1999.
Bernard Lewis, *The Middle East*, New York, Scribner, 1995.
Bernard Lewis, *What Went Wrong*, London, Weidenfeld and Nicholson, 2002.
John L. Esposito, *The Islamic Threat*, New York, The Oxford Press, 1999.
Samuel P. Huntington, *The Clash of Civilizations and the Remaking of World Order*, London, Touchstone Books, 1997.
Benjamin R. Barber, *Jihad Versus McWorld*, New York, Ballentine Books, 1992.
Thomas Friedman, *Miscellaneous Op-Ed Pieces*, *New York Times*, 2002, 2003.

· Norman Finkelstein, *The Holocaust Industry*, New York/ London, Verso, 2000.

As' ad AbuKhalil, Bin Laden, *Islam and America's New "War onTerrorism"*, New York, Seven Stories Press, 2002.

M. Faruk Zein, *Christianity, Islam and Orientalism*, London, Saqi Books, 2003.

The Jewish Virtual Library, www.us_Israel.org

The Palestine Center, www.PalestineCenter.org

Harry S. Truman, *Memoirs*, Garden City, N.Y., Doubleday and Company, 1956.

The Avalon Project, www.yale.edu/lawweb/Avalon/un

Henry Cattan, Palestine, *The Road to Peace*, London, Longman Group, 1971.

Fareed Zakaria, *The Future of Freedom*, New York/ London, W.W. Horton & Company, 2003.

UNRWA Website – www.un.org/unrwa

Tom Segev, *One Palestine, Complete*, New York, Henry Holt & Company, 2001.

Oliver James, *Prisoners of Circumstance*, Author House, 2001.

Human Rights Watch - Annual Report, 2003.

The New York Times

The International Herald Tribune

The University of Texas Libraries

About the Author

Oliver James is a retired executive of a major international corporation, now resident in southern Connecticut. The first ten years of his career were spent in the aviation industry, six of which in residence in Lebanon. After a break to return to school he worked nearly 30 years in the field of petroleum and petrochemicals. Born in Kentucky, he has lived in numerous places around the world including an eight-year stint in Saudi Arabia, five years in London, three years in Mexico and eight years in Belgium where he had responsibility for his company's business in the Middle East and Africa. As chief executive officer for several overseas affiliates and holder of senior positions with outside commercial and charitable organizations he has come to know well a broad spectrum of senior businessmen and prominent government officials, both in the United States and in those countries where he has resided and which he has frequented.

The author holds an engineering degree from the University of Kentucky and advanced degrees in engineering from Rensselaer Polytechnic Institute and in management from M.I.T. He has served in the army, both as an enlisted man and as an officer. Other publications include a novel set in the Middle East, *Prisoners of Circumstance*, and a responsible driving manual entitled *Driving According To Oliver*.

Printed in the United States
57301LVS00002B/182

9 781424 139286